Anonymous

Wax Flowers

How to make them

Anonymous

Wax Flowers
How to make them

ISBN/EAN: 9783337107024

Printed in Europe, USA, Canada, Australia, Japan

Cover: Foto ©ninafisch / pixelio.de

More available books at **www.hansebooks.com**

HOW TO MAKE THEM.

WITH

*NEW METHODS OF SHEETING WAX,
MODELLING FRUIT, &c.*

BOSTON:
J. E. TILTON AND COMPANY.
1864.

Entered, according to Act of Congress, in the year 1864, by
J. E. TILTON & CO.,
In the Clerk's Office of the District Court of the District of Massachusetts.

ELECTROTYPED AT THE
Boston Stereotype Foundry,
No. 4 Spring Lane.

PRINTED BY
GEO. C. RAND & AVERY, 3 CORNHILL.

CONTENTS.

	PAGE
INTRODUCTION.	7

WAX FRUIT.

Making Moulds of Two Parts,	12
Mould for an Orange,	12
Moulds for Lemons, Citrons, Limes, Melons, Capsicums, &c.,	17
Moulds for Plums, Apples, Pears, Cherries, Closed Peas, &c.,	18
Moulds of Peaches, Apricots, Filberts, Walnuts, Almonds, &c.,	20
Moulds for Half Fruit,	20
Moulds of Many Parts,	22
Moulds of the Pomegranate and Medlar,	22
Mould of a Cucumber and an Egg,	24
Mould of a Mulberry, Raspberry, &c.,	26
Pine Apple,	27
Section of Fruit,	28
Moulds of Small Fruit,	29
Grapes, Currants,	29
Other Objects,	29

CASTING THE FRUIT.

Casting an Orange,	31
Casting other Fruit,	32
Stalks,	34
Solid Fruit,	34

FINISHING THE FRUIT.

To Prepare the Fruit previous to Coloring,	36
Coloring Sections of Fruit,	38
Putting on a Rosy Tint,	40
Putting on Streaks, Specks, and Irregular Patches,	40
To put a Downiness or Powdering upon Fruit,	42
Varnishing a Fruit,	43

SMALL CLUSTERED FRUITS.

Not made by Casting nor in Wax,	45
To make Dark Grapes,	45
To make White Grapes,	47
To make Currants,	47
General Observations on Casting Wax,	48
Elastic Moulds,	49
To Obtain and Prepare Wax,	51
To Whiten Wax,	52
To Clean a Brush,	52
To Remove Wax from a Dress,	53

WAX FLOWERS.

Articles and Materials required,	54
Making Sheets of Wax,	55
White,	56
Yellow,	57
Pinks and Reds,	58
Blues,	58
Greens,	58
Colors required,	62
White and Green Down,	62
Brushes,	63
Patterns and Shapes,	64
Stamens and Pointal,	66
To make Waxen Leaves,	67
To make Succulent Stems, Buds, &c.,	68

MODELLING SIMPLE FLOWERS, 69

SINGLE AND SIMPLE FLOWERS.

The Snowdrop, Crocus, Primrose, and Violet,	72
The Crocus Tribe,	76
Crocus Sativus,	78
The Snowdrop,	79
The Violet,	80
The Heartsease,	82
The Tulip, Hyacinth, and Narcissus,	83
The Van Trol, or Sweet-scented Early Spring Tulip,	84
The Hyacinth,	85
The Narcissus,	88
The Pink, Jessamine, Daisy, Forget-me-not, Coreopsis, &c.,	93

CONTENTS.

The Single P ,	94
The Double k,	95
Clove and Carnation,	95
The Jasmine,	96
The Daisy,	97
The Forget-me-not,	98
The Coreopsis,	98
The Cyclamen,	99
Other Simple Flowers,	100
The Laburnum,	101
The Convolvulus,	101
The Fuchsia,	102
Engraving of a large Fuchsia,	105
Various Parts of the Fuchsia of the Natural Size,	106
Bell Flowers,	107
The Tobacco,	107
Honeysuckle,	107
The Poppy,	107
The Passion Flower,	108
The Single Rose,	110
The Chrysanthemum, China Aster, and other Quilled Flowers,	110
The Lily of the Valley,	112
MODELLING OF DOUBLE FLOWERS,	114

THE ART OF MODELLING WAX FLOWERS, FRUITS, &c.

HERE are no imitations of natural objects more exact and pleasing than those made of wax, more especially the representations of Fruit and Flowers. So exact, indeed, are they, that if well made, the most practised eye cannot sometimes detect the real from the artificial.

In Fruit, the choicest specimens of every clime may be thus assembled in a single vase, in all their apparent lusciousness and perfection; while in their waxen prototypes, lovely Flowers may be viewed in all their gorgeous coloring and transparent delicacy. As ornaments to the drawing-room, when grouped with taste, and blended with harmonic contrast, these waxen objects are not to be surpassed, whether we look at them as records of foreign productions seldom seen, — of extraordinarily beautiful specimens of home-growth, — of favorites which it is desirable to preserve, — or merely as beauties of ordinary production, which the eye delights to rest upon. Indeed, all lovers of flowers (and who are not?) must admire these, — their lovely *images*, transparent, vivid, and brilliant as they are.

The very beauty of waxen fruit and flowers, induces the belief that to make them must be difficult. "I can never make any so beautiful as these," is a very oft-repeated expression upon witnessing even a single group. Yet, in truth, no art is of more easy attainment; a little patience, and a little taste, are the whole mental requisites; these, superadded to ordinary care in the manipulation, cannot fail very shortly to render proficient the most inexperienced. Yet it is not to be denied, that a slight knowledge of the harmony of colors and of botany will greatly assist in the perfection of the more difficult of these works of elegance. The chief thing is to know *how to select the proper materials,* and *how to set about the work in a proper manner;* and, it may be added, to commence with what is most easy. Should it be a fruit, let it be one of a single color,—as an orange or a lemon; or, if a flower, we might recommend a snowdrop, a violet, or a narcissus, in which there is no complexity, and little pencilling.

In our larger cities, the requisite materials can always readily be procured, and it is not worth while that any of them should be home-made; yet, as persons who desire to practise this art may live far in the country, where it is difficult to obtain even the simpler requisites; and, as circumstances often arise in which it is absolutely impossible to procure what may be wanted for a particular purpose, as in the case of a mould being required for a certain specimen of a fruit, or the extra thick wax desirable for particular flowers, &c., we intend to include in this, our little book, every available information; that the learner, however remotely situated may be his residence, or unique his model, may have as much as possible his difficulties removed, his mind stimulated, and his fingers directed to attain excellence.

Beginning with the easiest department, it is necessary to divide the subject into the making of Fruit, and the making of Flowers. These are quite distinct in themselves; the former includes the imitation of all solid objects, with melted wax poured into moulds. The latter includes those more delicate ones, which are made without moulds, of wax previously cut into thin sheets.

WAX FRUIT.

THE art of making Wax Fruit includes every small object made in a mould; thus the same instructions that direct to make an orange, are equally applicable to form an egg, a pea, a cucumber, the stem of a cactus or stapelia, a doll, a bust, or any similar article, observing that the principle upon which all are formed is, that a mould is requisite. This is first to be made or procured, then wax is to be cast in it; sometimes solid, sometimes hollow. In many cases the objects will now be completely finished, with the exception of just trimming around where the mould joined; in other cases, the wax-castings are to be painted with dry colors for some, and wet colors for others; and in different manners, according to the effect desired to be produced. Thus the imitation of solid objects in wax

necessarily resolves itself into three distinct portions, each of which we must consider in detail; and first, as to

MAKING MOULDS OF TWO PARTS.

The materials and implements requisite for making the proper moulds are plaster of Paris; some slips of stiff paper, or ribbons of tin cut from thin tin-plates of their full length, and about three inches wide; some damp sand in a bowl; a pint basin; large spoon; small dinner-knife; and jug of water. The plaster of Paris should be quite fresh, and of good quality, superfine if it can be procured; it may be bought of any of the Italian figure-makers. Thus provided, procure a regularly formed fruit, and one which is neither hard like a walnut, nor yet rough like a peach, nor irregular like a pine-apple; an orange is a very good one for this purpose; then proceed as follows:—

Mould for an Orange.— Sink nearly one half the orange into the sand which has been previously damped; and it will be better, for a reason afterwards explained, to sink that part of the orange to which the stalk was attached, so that the widest part of the orange shall be just above the sand. Make the sand smooth around it. Then take one of the longest pieces of tin, bend it round into a hoop a little more than an inch wider than the orange, and keep it of this form and size by a bit of string tied round it, stick this hoop in the sand so as to enclose the orange, and be at an equal distance from it on every side, the upper edge of the tin standing up above the fruit, which is now prepared for casting from. If you have no tin, a piece of stiff and smooth brown paper, folded double, and one end fastened to the other by a wafer or wax, and the slip then made to surround the fruit, will do as well as the tin, though it is more troublesome to insert into the sand.

' Now prepare the plaster of Paris, which is to be poured on to the fruit. First pour water into the basin (it may be half or three quarters full), sprinkle the plaster into the water quickly, till it comes up to the top of the water, or till you think you have enough to cover the exposed half of the fruit to half an inch in depth, pour off the superfluous water, and stir the whole together quickly, till well mixed, to about the consistence of thick cream or honey; then pour the mixed plaster upon the fruit, so as to cover it all over equally, or as nearly so as possible, the plaster will, of course, be stopped from running away by the tin edging. If it should be too thin, and therefore run too much off the fruit, so as to leave the top bare, or nearly so, you must, after pouring it on the fruit, watch till it begins to harden, and then with a knife plaster it on the deficient parts, or else quickly mix up a little more to pour on; the whole of this must not take up above a minute or two, or the plaster will begin to *set*, as it is called; that is, it will commence solidifying, for it is the property of calcined plaster of Paris to unite itself with water with so strong a chemical affinity, that from an impalpable powder it becomes a hard and solid substance.

While the half mould, now roughly formed, is becoming hard enough to handle, the basin and spoon must be carefully washed, ready for use again presently, for a second quantity of plaster must never be mixed up in any vessel, till all former quantities be carefully washed away; and be it remarked, also, that if plaster gets hard and dry in a basin, spoon, or other vessel, the best way to remove it is to pour in a little water, when it will readily separate in one piece.

We will now suppose the plaster, which has been poured on the fruit, to have gotten about as hard as the flesh of a soft pear, or just hard enough to handle; when this is the case, take the whole up from the sand, take away with the point of the knife all sand which will drop from it, carefully remove the tin rim, and hold the mould by the fruit; now cut away any superfluous parts around the outside with a knife as quickly as convenient, for it is now momentarily getting harder; turn it up, and holding the mould itself in the hand, fruit uppermost, remove the orange, if it can be done readily without hurting the mould. Lay the fruit aside, cut away the lower edge of the mould where it has touched the sand, till the mould is exactly that of half the fruit, which is easily seen, by the shape of it internally. This is somewhat important, in order that the second half of the mould shall fit the fruit. If the tin has been of proper size, the mould will be half an inch thick around the edge.

The next operation is to prepare the second half of the mould, and that is easier and quicker to do than the first. First make two, three, or four holes with the round point of the knife in different parts of the edge of the former half, to such a depth and of such a size, that each will hold half a small marble or large pea. Then grease with tallow and salad oil, melted together in equal proportions, and laid on with a small brush, the edge of the finished half, holes and all. Wipe the orange from all sand, and place it in the half mould exactly as it came out, so that it shall fit in every part; surround the finished half mould with a long slip of stiff paper or tin, which you must tie on with a string, or fasten with a wafer. Place the whole, thus prepared, on a table or flat surface, fruit uppermost; prepare some more liquid plaster, as in the former instance, pour it upon the fruit, and let it partly harden. Then take off the edging, trim up

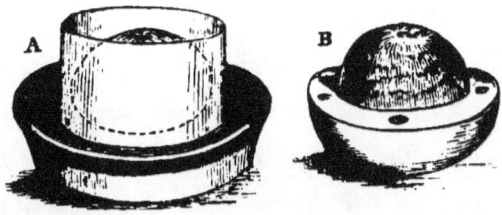

The cut above shows the moulding of the orange. A, represents it half buried in the sand, with the tin or paper around; B, is a view of the first half mould when complete.

the outside, and when quite hard, insert the blade of the knife between the two halves and separate them. The whole mould will now be complete, and the fruit being taken out, it will be ready to cast in.

This is the simple process employed for making two-part moulds of all equally or regularly formed fruit of the nature of the orange, or such as are at the same time soft and yielding, such as are without depressions, or irregular hollows or warts, and of such a nature that the plaster will not stick to them. For other fruit, as presently to be observed, a rather different method must be pursued.

If a second mould be desired of the same fruit, a new half may be cast from the fruit for either side of it, by the same method as pursued for the second half of the original mould, without having recourse to the sand, as in making the first.

Moulds for Lemons, Citrons, Limes, Melons, Capsicums, &c. — The moulds of all these may be made as explained for the orange, observing only, that a long fruit should be laid in the sand lengthways, and a round fruit stalkways; so that the joints of the mould shall for a lemon go from end to end; and for an orange round the greatest circumference, or round what we may call its equator. Sometimes a citron is so rough, that it will not deliver; that is, draw out of the mould, unless the latter be made of three pieces instead of two. Lemons, also, have very often a hollow next to the end knob, and, it may be, small knobs upon them; the largest or most irregular of these should be placed either quite downwards, or quite upwards in forming the moulds.

Moulds for Plums, Apples, Pears, Cherries, Closed Peas, Nectarines, Strawberries, Gooseberries, Green Figs, &c. — These are all fruit either too unyielding to be removed from the first half mould by pressure, as in the orange, or too soft not to be spoiled by the operation. The difference then to be observed in making the moulds for these and similar objects is only this, that the edge of the first half mould, where it touches the sand, is to be trimmed to exactly the half of the fruit, before the latter can be removed from it. It must be evident that every mould must divide in the widest part of the fruit, for if the fruit be sunk too much in the sand, the first half will not enclose enough of it, so if the first half be cut away too much, the second half will, in like manner, enclose too much, and the fruit being somewhat yielding, it may be removed, yet the wax cast afterwards to be withdrawn will be caught by the overhanging edges of the larger part of the mould, and the whole be spoiled, except that as the wax shrinks a little in cooling, if the difference of the two be but trifling, it may perhaps deliver, especially if the fruit be large as a melon. In making moulds of Strawberries, Figs, and other soft fruit, great care must be taken in their removal, for if they are broken, they cannot be replaced well to make the second half. The calyx of the strawberry must be removed before making the mould, and a little piece of dough, putty, or cotton-wool be put into the hole where the centre piece is drawn out along with the calyx; if it should be so, though this should be avoided if possible. Egg Plums have mostly a channel down them, this should be at the bottom of the mould. Greengages, and many other Plums, Nectarines, most

A, represents the first half mould of an apple in section, intended to show the nature of the small connecting holes; B, is the first half of a pear, showing its lengthways position.

Apples, Cherries, &c., have a deep hollow or depression where the stalk grows; in all these cases the stalk should be removed, and this part placed downwards in the sand; also be careful, if there is any defect in the fruit, as a hole pecked by a bird, a speck of decay, an injury, or curious growth, that this part shall be so placed, that neither the mould nor the fruit shall be torn away in the removal of one from the other. Imperfect fruit is by no means to be rejected as unworthy of imitation; on the contrary, it is generally more natural than the unblemished specimens. The stalks of long Pears may be left on the fruit; they will deliver well if laid lengthways in the sand.

Moulds of Peaches, Apricots, Filberts, Walnuts, Almonds, &c. — No instruction is requisite for these fruits beyond the above, except that as the plaster will stick to them, either on account of their hairiness or their dry hardness, it is requisite to grease them well before placing them in the sand; and as the grease will cause the sand to adhere to them, after separating the first half mould, let them be well cleaned from sand before they are placed in it for the second cast; when thus placed, it is usual to grease well with the oil and tallow, both the fruit and edge of the mould at the same time.

MOULDS FOR HALF FRUIT.

It is often desired to form a model of a Half Apple, Pear, or Peach. This is very easily done. First consider where the section shall be, and either tie a thread round the fruit at this place, or else mark it round with a knife, just cutting through the rind; a thread is best for an Orange, Lemon, or Peach, and a cut for an Apple or Pear. Insert almost all the part which is to be cut off, and which should, in a two-part mould, be always half, or more than half the fruit, into the sand; make a half mould upon it as before directed, trim up this, remove the fruit, trim up the edge of the mould to the line before marked out, or rather beyond it, make the proper holes to connect it with the next half, grease the edge well, put the fruit in its place so as to fit exactly, then cut it through, leaving of course half in; see that the pips are properly in their places; if apple-pips, pear-pips, or the dry stones of plums or apricots, oil them a little, then, having fastened around the already finished half mould a paper edge or guard, pour the mixed plaster over the cut half, and it will be the exact counterpart of it. In removing this when set, it is very probable that the pips will adhere to it, or may even be imbedded in it; in this case, cut away carefully with a penknife, till you come down to them, when they may be removed. To take a section of a fruit, as three quarters of an apple, a portion of a melon, &c., will be described in the next division of the subject, viz. :—

MOULDS OF MANY PARTS.

These moulds are somewhat more difficult to form than those before described, though the same general principles are to be regarded, and the same manipulation in most respects preserved. These three or four-part moulds are applicable to all fruits, and other objects of such a form that they cannot be divided into two halves; or if so divided, there remain little knobs, depressions, or irregularities, that will not readily remove from the mould. The Pine Apple will afford an illustration of fruit for which a sectional mould will be necessary. The following remarks upon various objects of this kind, added to the preceding instructions, will render equally familiar the making moulds more complex than those hitherto described.

Moulds of the Pomegranate and Medlar. — The Pomegranate, which is produced from a splendid crimson flower, is well known to be a hard-shelled fruit. The stalk end of this flower expands afterwards into the fruit, while the other end, the outer part of which forms at first a five-cleft calyx, remains attached, and becomes hard like the rest of the fruit. In making a mould of a perfect fruit then, this part must be carefully preserved, and imitated in the model; and it is necessary to make first a mould of this part, as if distinct from the rest. To do this, first grease the fruit well around the top, then tie round the calyx here alluded to a piece of paper as an edging, pour into this some mixed plaster, first resting the fruit upright; it will be caught by the paper, and mould the top of the fruit. When hard, trim it up a little, cutting all away which comes on the outside of the five-leaved calyx, leave it an inch projecting on the top, and cut this to the shape shown at A. In this piece it will be seen that there is a cross notch, or a hole which will do as well, the object of which is to show better how it fits the parts afterwards to be made.

This part being made, grease it well on one half, as well as the fruit itself for one half or more, lay it thus greased, nearly half buried in the sand, as if for making a two-part mould, taking care that no part above the sand shall have been left ungreased. Then proceed, as before directed, to form two half moulds, burying up, in so doing, the plug which was first formed, and if it has been cut to a proper shape, it will at times be held fast in its place when the mould is empty. Sometimes the part of the calyx remaining on the ripe fruit is so closed up, or united together, that it is not necessary to take this trouble, but in this case the mould may be made in two parts, like those of the apple or pear.

The open calyx of the Medlar requires the same method to be pursued as recommended for the pomegranate, and the fruit being rough, requires also greasing. An unripe medlar is the easiest to cast from, but a ripe and much bruised one is the most natural. It is seldom that a medlar is made in wax.

Mould of a Cucumber and an Egg. — The mould of a Cucumber is usually of three parts, as the knobs upon it will not allow it to be drawn from a two-part mould. We premise, of course, that a person would usually choose a long, bent, and irregular Cucumber to imitate; with such a one, proceed as follows:—Bury it in the sand, so that rather more than one third of it remain above, then place the tin around it (and here a great advantage is found in tin over paper, it bending readily to the shape of the Cucumber), yet it may happen that two lengths of tin are necessary; if so, place them so as to overlap each other, and put a piece of string around them, if necessary, to keep them together; mix and pour the plaster, let it get partly hard, remove the tin, take up the mould and fruit, and trim the former, so that it shall be the mould of about one third of the fruit, and make the proper connection holes, as before directed. A cross section of this part finished is shown at A in the cut. Next grease rather more than half this new formed third mould, and put it perpendicularly sideways, fruit and all, into the sand, as shown at B. Surround the fruit part of it with the tin, so that when the plaster is next poured, it shall cover half or rather more of the unmoulded part of the fruit, being stopped on one side by the tin, and on the other by the first part formed. Take it up when set enough, remove the two moulds from the fruit, and trim up the newly-formed piece, taking care that you do not break or disturb the edge which adjoins the other mould. When trimmed, grease the new piece, put it with the former piece over the fruit, and grease the other edge of the first formed piece, surround the whole with paper or tin, and pour the plaster upon it as before. When set, it may be taken apart, and the fruit taken out. The three parts united will form a perfect mould of the Cucumber. The mould, before the last addition has been made to it, will resemble in section the cut at C. A longitudinal mould in its first stage is seen at D.

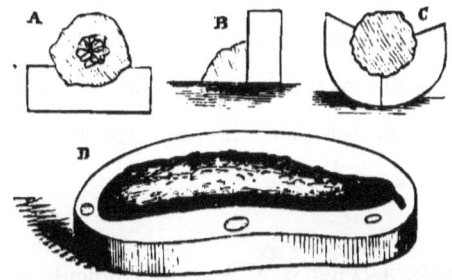

An Egg had better be moulded in three pieces, as it will seldom deliver well in two pieces. This object being always procurable, and less unyielding than a Cucumber, is an easy and good object to practise upon.

Mould of a Mulberry, Raspberry, &c.—These fruits require to be moulded in the same way as the Cucumber. Sometimes, however, the Raspberry may be made in two pieces; in this case one half must enclose the point of it up to the thickest part, and the other, the stalk end, to meet the former. When made in three parts, the first part should enclose the stalk end of the fruit up to the thickest part of it, and the other two moulds should be made sideways. A Mulberry should be made in four pieces, each containing a quarter, and so placed as to confine the fruit from end to end. No moulds are more troublesome than those of the mulberry and raspberry, on account of the soft pulpy character of the fruit, and the consequent difficulty of trimming up the moulds properly, or removing them; also, if bruised, the juice is very apt to impair the strength of the mould.

Pine Apple. — This is a fruit not difficult to mould, although it requires four or more pieces. First, cut off the stalk and pull out the top leaves; bury the whole of the fruit in sand, except a circle of about two and a half or three inches at the top or leafy end, pour plaster on this part after slightly oiling it, and surrounding it with tin; let it set, take off this plaster piece from the fruit, trim it up, and be careful not to cut the edge where it touched the sand in a straight line, but in notches, so as to agree with the square or irregular portions which the fruit itself consists of, and which for this part will be seen very readily, by the irregularities of the mould itself. It need only be cut thus towards the inner part. You will not forget to make four or five, or even more, holes with the point of the knife around this foot or end mould, to connect it well with the pieces afterwards cast. This part being greased, put it again upon the Pine Apple, and the latter being cleaned from sand, place the two together lengthways in the sand, leaving rather more than one quarter above. Cast this upper quarter as before directed; trim it up, grease it, and cast adjoining this and the foot mould, a second quarter of the fruit, then the third, and afterwards a completing one, forming altogether five pieces. A string had better be tied round the four sectional moulds to keep them together. Some Pine Apples mould much better than others.

Sections of Fruit. — The manner of making moulds for straight sections of common fruits has already been described. For other sections, as when a quarter is cut from a melon, or one third of an apple or an orange, the moulds had better be of three parts, the part cut out forming the first part cast, and for this we need only surround the fruit with a piece of paper, tying it on; it must be put in the sand to cast the second piece.

Moulds of Small Fruit. — Small fruit, such as Strawberries, Raspberries, &c., are generally cast solid; the method pursued for larger fruit being scarcely applicable to them. It is therefore requisite to bore a hole through one portion of the mould to pour the melted wax in. This hole should taper downwards like a funnel, and must be made at such a part that it will not injure the appearance of the fruit; for example, at the stalk end of the fruit, as it will in the strawberry, &c., be hidden by the calyx afterwards to be put over it. The hole to pour the wax in should not be made in the Cherry, as the fruit is so smooth and shiny that it is very difficult to hide the place.

Grapes, Currants, and other fruit of the like kind, is never moulded, but made by glass balls, as afterwards described.

Other Objects. — In the same manner that the moulds of fruit are made, may be made moulds of many other objects, as stems and leaves of many of the Cactuses, Stapelias, and other succulent plants, — radishes, onions, confectionery articles, dolls and figures, moulds for the electrotype, &c.

3 *

CASTING THE FRUIT.

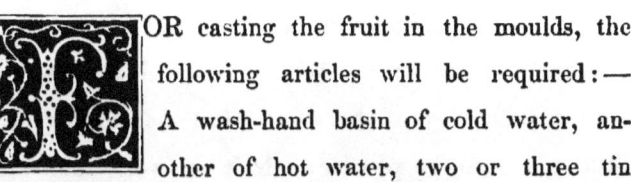

FOR casting the fruit in the moulds, the following articles will be required:— A wash-hand basin of cold water, another of hot water, two or three tin saucepans, or other vessels, with spouts, to melt the wax in, a towel, and the following colors in fine powder, or, better still, ground in oil, such as artists use, and which are usually sold by the tube, viz., light chrome yellow, lake, Prussian blue, and raw umber; also, some red lead in powder, and a sufficiency of wax. The best wax is not necessary, the remaining pieces of half-burnt wax or composition candles will do equally well, besides which, the wicks of the candles is the best material for the stalks of many fruit. A bone knife or a teaspoon is also necessary to stir up the melted wax. Thus furnished, set to work as follows: The method being exactly the same for every fruit which is to be cast hollow; the color alone differs, and this must be always in accordance with the fruit, observing that the lightest color of the fruit is that to be imitated; the spots, darker tints, streaks, &c., are to be put on afterwards. First, we will commence with an orange.

Casting an Orange.—Prepare the mould by soaking it for ten minutes in water as hot as the hand can conveniently bear. While the mould is soaking, melt a sufficiency of the wax; when melted, put in a little red lead in powder; stir it up well; then take out the mould from the water, wipe it dry on the surface, but without rubbing it, lest you should rub out the fine irregularities on the inside of the mould, which constitute the beauty of the fruit. The mould will now be penetrated with water, but without having the surface wet, thus preventing the wax sticking to it. Thus ready, hold one half the mould in the left hand, nearly fill this half side with the melted wax just stirred up, taking care that none of it has run over the edge or joint, put the other half of the mould on it, squeeze the two pieces tight together with the hands, and still holding them tight, turn them over and over in every manner, so that the melted wax shall, before it congeals, pass equally over the whole internal surface of the mould. The mould being warm with the water, and still further warmed by the wax, it would take perhaps ten minutes before the whole were congealed; to save time, you must have recourse to the basin of cold water, and dip your hands and the mould in the water, still turning it about, thus keeping it immersed, and turning it for two or three minutes, the wax will have become hard, which may be known by shaking it, and the same time listening whether there is the sound of a liquid within. If set, leave it to rest for a few minutes in the cold water. Then the halves of the mould may be pulled off, and the orange will be found perfect in form, and of a natural color. The only thing now to be done is to take off with a penknife any mark of the joint of the mould, and if the knife itself leaves a mark, smooth it off with a bit of rag, damped with turpentine.

Casting other Fruit. — The other fruit, which require no after-coloring, or which are finished when cast and trimmed up, are the Walnut, Lemon, and perhaps some others. For the Lemon, the wax is to be colored with chrome yellow; for the Walnut and Medlar, raw umber

may be added to it; for the pomegranate and chestnut, burnt umber is better. The Strawberry, Raspberry, and Cherry may be cast white, or some of them lake and white. The Egg Plum, and several of the Pears and Apples, may be yellow. The innumerable shades of green may be formed of different admixtures of chrome yellow and Prussian blue. For the Mulberry and dark Plums, use Prussian blue and lake, in different proportions. The pine apple is to be yellow; the banana a dark green or a yellow, according to the sort or ripeness of the fruit. Gooseberries of various colors, — for the dark-red gooseberry, you may mix together lake with a little raw or burnt umber. Filberts are to be cast green; so are Melons. Quinces, a bright yellow. Greengage Plums, a very light bluish green. *All fruit, of which a part is cut off, is to be cast of the color of the inner flesh, which is seen;* of the Orange, this is yellow; of the Apple, white; of the Melon, salmon-colored, made by red lead and chrome yellow; in this case, notwithstanding the general direction, the Melon had better be cast green, and the flesh painted. Of the Pomegranate, the seeds within are seen to be a fine scarlet. The colors of other fruit will easily suggest themselves.

Stalks. — All moulds which have been made with the stalks of the fruit remaining, and these are chiefly Peas, Cucumbers, or, in a few cases, Apples, must have these stalks on the part where the moulds join, and, in casting, or rather previous to casting, a piece of twisted cotton, with a wire in it, must be laid in the proper part, so as to project into the fruit; when the latter is cast, the cotton will be fixed to its place. Stalks that are put in after the fruit is cast, will meet with our attention hereafter, as it does not belong to the casting.

Solid Fruit. — Small fruit cannot be well cast in the above manner. The best process, then, is to tie parts of the mould together, and pour the wax through a hole at the top, until the mould is full; then place this in cold water, but not so that the water can run into the hole at the top; let it stop a minute, then pour out again all the wax not congealed, so that the fruit will be solid or not, according to the management pursued.

FINISHING THE FRUIT.

FTER the wax fruit are cast, they require first to have the mark or ridge left by the joints of the mould carefully pared off with a penknife, and then generally the knife-marks smoothed off with a small piece of rag dipped in turpentine or spirits of wine; very numerous fruits will, after this simple operation, be quite finished, as the Orange, Lemon, Walnut, and all other fruits which are of uniform color. The beauty, however, of most fruits, lies not merely in their shape, but upon a correct imitation of their bloom, rosiness, down, streaks, specks, and so on; and in imitating these properly consists the only difficulty of wax-fruit making. The materials now required are various colors, as carmine in powder, together with the same colors used in casting; also,

there will be required a small piece of flannel, two or three camel's hair brushes, thin wire covered with green silk for the stalks of Cherries, and a little green paper colored on both sides, for the calyx of Strawberries and Raspberries, a few cloves for the flower end of an apple, a bottle of mastic varnish, some powder blue for the bloom of Plums and Grapes, and some white or yellowish down for the mealiness of Greengages, Peaches, &c.; this is of three kinds, one is arrow-root, this is the most inferior; the second is paper powder, made by scraping white paper away with a penknife; the third is white flock, procured at the paper stainers, or it may be made by cutting up into a very fine powder a piece of fine kerseymere, or other fine wollen cloth, and sifting the cuttings.

To Prepare the Fruit previous to Coloring. — The cast having been trimmed up, sometimes requires to be stalked, &c. Pears, Melons, Cucumbers, &c., as already observed, may generally be cast with the stalks on, using the cotton wicks of the wax candles, cut to twice the intended length, and with a piece of wire inserted in each. Apples, Plums, Cherries, and some other fruits, should have this stalk inserted after the fruit is cast, and before it is colored. Some should have the stalk inserted last of all, as the Strawberry and the Raspberry. The stalk of the Apple, &c., may be made of wire covered with silk, and to give it a natural appearance, it may be dipped in melted wax. When thus made, thrust it into the proper part of the fruit. If the stalk does not hold fast, unroll the stalk for about a quarter of an inch, hold this part in the candle till the wax, which is over the silk, just begins to melt. Thrust it, while thus warm, into the fruit, which hold upside down, so that the stalk shall be lowest, till the wax around it is congealed. The stalk may afterwards be painted to imitate Nature more accurately. Apple, plum, and damson stalks are generally bent; cherry-stalks two inches long, and nearly straight. The eye end of an apple, pear, and quince, has the remains of a five-leaved calyx which once enclosed the flower. This is very readily imitated by the spice called a clove. Put one of these on the bar or hob of a stove to get hot; then, while hot, thrust it into the apple, holding the fruit that side downwards till set hard. Some persons dip these cloves into the melted wax of the same color as the fruit previous to inserting them. To do this conveniently, a needle or pin is thrust into the head of the clove previous to dipping, that it may not soil the fingers. When the cloves are dipped, there should be a hole made for their reception, otherwise the wax will be borne up as they are thrust down, occasioning a disagreeable appearance, and which superfluity is not very readily removed without disturbing the clove. Observe that stalks are always to be made of a green color at first, unless cast with the fruit, as in the case of a pear, when they may be cast yellow like the pear itself. All of the orange tribe have very dark stalks; it is only young oranges that should have stalks. The cherry stalk is formed light green, and tinted darker afterwards by rubbing over it a little brown in powder.

Coloring Sections of Fruit. — The internal part of fruit is generally, if not always, of a very different color from the exterior. Thus the outside of the Walnut is brown, the kernel white, or with its skin on it cream color. The rind of an Orange is much darker than the pulp. The flesh of an Apple or Pear is generally white, while the peel is yellow, brown, or green. In casting a section in wax, a difficulty may arise from these causes; yet a little thought and patience will readily overcome it. The fruit, if cast all at one time, should generally be cast of the lighter color, and the other color painted on afterwards, according to Nature; thus of the half orange, we should cast it yellow, and afterwards paint the pips (if visible) white, and the rind orange color, made chiefly of red lead. It is often advisable to cast the fruit in two sections. To do this, the following hints may suffice: First, take the flat part of the mould, or that which represents the flesh; pour upon it a little wax, colored of the proper tint, trim it so as to take away any films of wax that would interfere with the joint of the two moulds when put together; then partly fill the other or deeper side of the mould with the different color for the rind, unite the two together, and turn them about till the whole wax is set, as before directed. The cast will now be complete as to the colors of the two parts. A Walnut will have two deep moulds, one of the half shell, the other of the half kernel of the opposite part of the nut. First, cast the kernel side, to the open half mould; fill the mould with the cream-colored wax, not made too hot; when a little set, pour out what is not wanted; cut it clean across the edge. Next, nearly fill the other half mould with brown wax, unite the two together, turn them about, and let it settle with the shell side downwards; a fine and natural cast is obtained by this means. If you desire to cast walnuts solid, let the hole, where the wax is to be poured in, be in the middle of one of the shells. Upon this principle the sections of all fruit may be cast in very nearly their proper colors, whether the sections be of a piece cut off, or a piece cut out.

Putting on a Rosy Tint. — The fine scarlet hues of ripeness are very easily put on; indeed, as easily as a lady of ancient days would rouge her cheeks, and in much the same manner; all that is requisite, is to take up a little of the powdered carmine on a small piece of flannel, and rub it gently and regularly over such part of the fruit as is to be thus ornamented; it will soon communicate all the effect desired. The bloom may thus be given to the Newton Pippin and many other apples, to the white-heart Cherry, some of the summer Pears, the Peach and Apricot, and very slightly to the green and yellow Plums.

Putting on Streaks, Specks, and Irregular Patches. — All these things must be done with the proper colors, mixed with mastic varnish, spirit varnish, or turpentine, and sprinkled or else laid on with a sable or camel's hair brush. To accomplish this with facility and truth, a little practice, guided by observation and taste, will effect more than the most minute instructions. Indeed, it is like painting in general, so purely a mechanical process, that all we could say upon the matter would be almost useless. The beauties and blemishes, whichever they may be, that constitute the streaks and specks upon fruit, are almost always scarlet or carmine, the brown of raw umber, or some mixture of these two. For ribstone Pippins, and some other apples, lake is to be preferred to carmine; white-heart Cherries, when over-ripe, have irregular specks or patches of brown upon them. The green and yellow Plums, green Grapes, Apricots, and Peaches have specks more or less crimson, tempered a little with brown. The decay spots of apples and pears are brown only, the streaks of ripeness are red. Irregular spottiness may be produced thus: Mix carmine or other color with turpentine, spirits of wine, or varnish, so as to be very weak of color; take up a little in a hard tinting brush, such as is used in coloring wax for flowers; hold this charged brush at a little distance, draw a pen through it, so as to spurt or sprinkle the color upon the fruit; it will of course lie in specks, and produce a good and natural effect. The effect is much heightened sometimes by putting a blush over the fruit first, or by wetting it with turpentine. The specks, by this means, flow, in some degree, into each other, become softened around their edges, or run partly into streaks. The seeds of a strawberry are colored by painting them with bright chrome yellow. A Chestnut is cast in raw umber, and colored with burnt umber.

To put a Downiness or Powdering upon Fruit. — One of the powders mentioned on the 36th page is adapted for this purpose. Suppose that you desire to put on the mealiness which is so visible upon a peach, you would first color one side of it with a red blush, to show the ripeness of that part which has been exposed to the sun, and which will generally be over one half of the fruit. This being done, take in the palm of the hand a small quantity of white or slightly yellow flock, put the fruit upon this, and roll it along with the flock between the hands, until sufficiently and equally covered with the fine woolly particles. It should be done over a sheet of paper, that none of the flock be wasted. If it is an Apricot to be covered, use an orange, or rather buff-colored flock, or else the white flock mixed with dark chrome yellow in powder. Dark Grapes and dark Plums are to be dusted over with powder blue from a muslin bag, and green grapes, plums, &c., with arrow-root in the same manner; but as the arrow-root has always a cold and raw appearance, and is too white to be natural, it is better to use hair powder, which has been rubbed up with a slight quantity of a greenish yellow powder of any kind.

If a person is not furnished with oil or powder colors, and dislikes the use of varnish or turpentine, he may use for all purposes of finishing the cast fruit the ordinary water colors of the paint-boxes, rubbed up in the customary way with water, to which a drop or two of ox-gall has been added. This last is necessary to make the colors adhere to the wax, which is of a greasy nature. It is to be observed, however, that fruit, &c., colored with water colors, cannot be washed, as that may which has been finished in turpentine or varnish.

Varnishing a Fruit. — There are few fruits that require to be varnished after having been painted, this finishes the process respecting them. The Lady Apple, a beautiful little American species, is always very glossy, so are all kinds of Cherries. Many fruits may be improved and rendered glossy by gently rubbing them with a flannel, and this rubbing is generally necessary in some degree with all fruit, but it is not sufficient with Cherries, Strawberries, Chestnuts, the seeds of an Apple or Pear, the flesh of a Pomegranate, Orange, or Apple. These and other things of the like kind are to have one coat of mastic varnish, laid on with a soft camel's hair brush as evenly as possible, so as to show no ridges. The varnish must not be laid on till the under-painting is quite dry, lest it should become smeared.

SMALL CLUSTERED FRUITS.

NOT MADE BY CASTING NOR IN WAX.

OME few Fruits are not made in wax at all, nor in moulds, and yet are of such a character as to add greatly to the appearance of a group or cluster. These are chiefly Grapes and Currants, and which are made with balls of glass tied together, of various sizes, so that in making a bunch of grapes, you may select the requisite variety of size. There are smaller round ones of the sizes for currants.

To make Dark Grapes. — First, choose three or four dozen bulbs from the smallest to the largest size. Next, cut a corresponding number of wires for stalks, about two inches long each; these should be made of a thin wire covered with green silk, of such a size that it will readily enter the mouth or hole of the glass bulb. Melt some wax, and color it purple with Prussian blue and lake, putting in more or less of the one or the other, according to the real color of the grape. These must be in a saucepan or dish, not less than an inch in depth. Dip one end of one of the intended stalks into this melted wax, and insert it into the mouth of the glass bulb, and hold it there for a minute, till it is well fixed by the congealing of the wax. Fasten the whole in the same manner. Now take up each grape separately by the stalk; dip the bulb part wholly into the wax; take it out instantly and turn it up, so that the stalk shall be underneath, and consequently any drop of wax there may be will settle around the stalk, and not on the bulb itself. In a minute or so, the grape having now a film of wax over its surface, will have all the semi-transparency of the real fruit. The whole being done in this way, tie them together in a natural manner by their stalks, observing to put the smallest grapes near to the bottom of the bunch. When tied together and naturally arranged, sprinkle slightly over them a little powder blue from a muslin bag. Finally, rub off with the finger some of this powder blue from the prominent parts, as if the grapes had been handled or rubbed in packing. The most natural way to do this, is to roll them between the hands.

To make White Grapes. — The only difference here is, that the wax used both for fastening on the stalks and for dipping the bulbs into, is colored a light yellowish green; and when finished, the grapes are to be very slightly dusted over with arrow-root or hair powder, or, for some grapes, no dusting is necessary.

To make Currants — There are ten or twelve Currants in a bunch, and these are made of bulbs similar to those for grapes. First, put short stalks to them of very fine green wire; dip them for White Currants into wax slightly tinged yellow; for Red Currants and Black Currants the same. The white will require no painting; the red and black must be colored with carmine, or with a dark purple, as their natural tint requires; then for the end opposite to the stalk, and where the flower has been, put a spot of black paint, or a minute bunch of black or brown wool; let them next be arranged loosely into a bunch, and finally varnished.

GENERAL OBSERVATIONS ON CASTING WAX.

The wax may be, and often is, congealed around the hole as well as the sides; in this case it is evident that the hole must be cleared, before the liquid within can escape; it is scarcely worth while to pour any out of a Cherry, Raspberry, Mulberry, or other similarly small object. In casting a large object through a hole, there should only be a small quantity of wax allowed to congeal first; in a few minutes a second coat may be poured in, and afterwards a third; this method will prevent cracking. The object of the water to soak the mould in at first and between each casting, is to prevent the wax and mould sticking together; and the reason hot water is preferred is, that it may not congeal the wax too rapidly. In a mould which is too cold, the wax will often settle in ridges or streaks. The mould, when filled, or partly filled, as the case may be, is, after such filling, plunged and turned about in cold water, merely to hasten the congealing of it. Wax should be melted always by a very slow and gentle heat; the heat of boiling water is always sufficient; thus a common glue pot is an excellent thing to melt it in. This is to be attended to for two reasons, one, because if too hot, it will be apt to adhere to the mould, and also because, when any color has been mixed with it, this color becomes darker; especially when there is chrome yellow in it, this turns by heat dark olive. If great toughness is required in a wax cast or mould, one ounce of yellow rosin, or still better, of Canada balsam, is to be added to every pound of wax. Wax moulds for plaster-casting or the electrotype should have the above, and also one fourth its weight of flake white and red lead, mixed together, previous to melting. Modelling wax, and that used for wax dolls, hair dresser's blocks, &c., are colored with flake white and vermilion, the latter in very small quantity.

Wax is sometimes adulterated with white lead, tallow, suet, potato starch, or rosin. When wax is bought, it is proper to break each cake, for it is not unfrequently the case that some impurities are in the centre, the outside only being good.

ELASTIC MOULDS.

The body to be moulded, previously oiled, must be secured one inch above the surface of a board, and then surrounded by a wall of clay, about an inch distant from its sides. The clay must also extend rather higher than the contained body: into this, warm melted glue, as thick as possible, so that it will run, is to be poured, so as to completely cover the body to be moulded; the glue is to remain till cold, when it will have set into an elastic mass, just such as is required.

Having removed the clay, good glue is to be cut into as many pieces as may be necessary for its removal, either by a sharp-pointed knife, or by having placed threads in the requisite situation of the body to be moulded, which may be drawn away when the glue is set, so as to cut it out in any direction. The portions of the glue mould having been removed from the original, are to be placed together and bound round by tape.

In some instances it is well to run small wooden pegs through the portions of the glue, so as to keep them exactly in their proper positions. If the mould be of considerable size, it is better to let it be bound with moderate tightness upon a board, to prevent it bending whilst in use; having done as above described, the wax is to be poured into the mould and left to set. The wax must not be poured in whilst too hot; as it cools so rapidly when applied to the cold glue, that the sharpness of the impression is not injured.

When the moulds are not used soon after being made, treacle should be previously mixed with the glue, to prevent its becoming hard.

The description thus given is with reference to casting those bodies which cannot be so well done by any other than an elastic mould; but glue moulds will be found greatly to facilitate casting in many departments, as a mould may be frequently taken by this method in two or three pieces, which would, on any other principle, require many.

TO OBTAIN AND PREPARE WAX.

The wax should be put in a moderately fine hair bag, well tied up, and be boiled briskly in a clean saucepan, with sufficient water to well cover the bag, and half an ounce of aqua-fortis to each quart of water; a weight should be placed upon the bag to keep it down. As the wax rises to the top of the water, it is to be skimmed off with a spoon, and be put into a pan, and when no more rises, the bag must be pressed by having a flat board and a heavy weight placed on it, to squeeze out any wax that may remain. The wax so obtained should be re-boiled in fresh water, and treated the same way as before, and even a third boiling may be necessary, in order to have it quite pure; after the last boiling, it is to be poured into moulds to form cakes. The quantity of aqua-fortis at the second boiling, may be reduced one half; and if it is boiled a third time, it may still further be reduced to the same extent. If wanted white, it is bleached.

TO WHITEN WAX.

The process of bleaching wax in order to give it that beautiful whiteness which it has in commerce, is effected generally by chemical means; but it may be bleached in small quantities as follows: Take the best and cleanest beeswax you can obtain, melt it in hot water, skim it off into a cup or basin, previously oiled, when quite cold, cut the wax into thin slices, expose these to the action of the sun and air upon white dishes, sprinkling it, unless there be rain, once or twice a day with clean water; at the end of a week melt the wax again, and proceed as before. In hot weather, the wax may be floated on water in the middle of the day, as it is best not to allow it to melt.

TO CLEAN A BRUSH

That has been in turpentine, wash it with hot water and soap; and if it has been used in varnish, cleanse it first in spirits of wine for spirit varnish, and turpentine for oil varnish, such as copal, mastic, &c. These are called oil varnishes, although made with turpentine.

TO REMOVE WAX FROM A DRESS.

It not unfrequently happens, that when wax is melted, some is spilt on the dress; it may be removed as follows: Toast the crumb of a small piece of bread, and, while hot, apply it to the droppings of wax, a portion of which it will absorb and take up, and by repeating this process, the whole wax will be gradually removed.

WAX FLOWERS.

O understand properly the making of Models of Flowers from Wax, we must first allude to the materials employed, then to the procuring of proper shapes or patterns, afterwards to the fashioning of these materials, cut to the required patterns into the object to be imitated; and finally, the natural arrangement and finishing of each part, the decorating it with artificial leaves, tendrils, &c., and the grouping of the whole together into a harmonious contrast.

ARTICLES AND MATERIALS REQUIRED.

The materials of which Imitative Flowers are made, are sheets of wax of many different colors, to form the petals, leaves, &c., and wire of different thicknesses covered with green silk. The articles used to fashion and color the flowers are curling pins, various dry and water colors, ox-gall, tinting brushes, camel's hair pencils, a pair of scissors to cut the wax, shapes of tin, card, or stiff paper; varnish for certain flowers; white and green down for dusting over such as appear mealy. If the waxen sheets are made at home, other trifling articles are necessary; this is always advisable with those who consume much wax, because the home-made sheets do not cost a quarter as much as those bought, and also because the person making these things herself, is able to procure, with accuracy, every tint required, and to make her wax of every size and thickness; indeed, we never knew an artist who could imitate successfully even the generality of flowers, much less the extraordinary ones, — as the Stapelias, the Orchideous plants, &c., who did not make for herself all the wax required. It is right, then, first to describe fully this process.

Making Sheets of Wax. — Have ready, at the commencement of the operation, about two pounds of white wax, a portion of Canada or fir balsam; the following colors, ground in oil, or else in a dry state; — chrome yellow, light and dark, Prussian blue, cobalt or French ultramarine (the former is the best), carmine and Chinese, or permanent white; these will make every tint required. You will want also a small saucepan with a lip, or, what is better, two saucepans, one to go readily into the other, in the manner of a glue-pot: a clean glue-pot is itself much to be preferred. The object of this double vessel is, that the outer one should have water put in it, while the inner vessel holds the wax, thus the latter being melted by the heat of boiling water only, never burns, boils over, or gets discolored;—there should be a cover over it. The next thing wanted is a square tin mould, made one inch deep, two and a half inches wide, and five or six long, made in the manner of a cake tin, with a wire around the top. This is all that is required for casting the wax first into blocks. You had first better make some white, because that color is more used than any other, and the scraps left will cast again for other colors; it will take half a pound of wax to fill the above sized mould, and the block thus made, will cut up into five or six dozen sheets or more. The vessel that holds the melted wax should be glazed porcelain or crockery, and should not be used, particularly if white wax is needed.

White. — Cast some transparent, and others a little opaque; the former will be made by putting half a pound of wax and one ounce of Canada or fir balsam into the saucepan; then, when melted, stirring it up well with a bone spoon, or a piece of wood, and pouring it into the mould, having first greased the mould, so as to allow it to be separated from the tin, it is then ready for cutting into sheets. If it is to be an opaque white, stir up with the wax, when melted, more or less of the permanent or Chinese white; pour it when of a uniform color. A very little white will suffice, as it must never be much colored. The wax, when ready for sheeting, should not be too hard; say, about the condition of new bar soap.

Yellow. — Mix with the transparent wax more or less chrome yellow, either light or dark, according to the tint required. There are generally four yellows made, — primrose color, light yellow, fit for certain carnations, roses, tulips, &c., dark yellow, as for the jonquil and orange.

Pinks and Reds. — Color with different quantities of carmine or Chinese vermilion. It may be made various shades. The first being excessively pale, fit for the blush rose; the two next, ordinary rose colors; and the darkest, which is a deep red, like the damask rose, various red hyacinths, &c.

Blues. — There are but two colors of blue wax usually made, one by a light blue, colored with cobalt, the other a full tint, formed of Prussian blue and wax. The first is for light-colored blue hyacinth, the other for dark hyacinths, and some of the companulas.

Greens. — There will be required six or seven different tints of green, from the light grass-green of the primrose leaf, to the deep green of the camellia, they are all colored by the different admixtures of light chrome yellow and Prussian blue or chrome green.

There are numerous other colors required, but they are produced by coloring the white wax by means afterwards described. This is chiefly because most flowers which are colored, are not alike on both sides, and are generally quite white towards the centre of the flower, and to use a colored wax for such a purpose, would be to give a muddiness that would entirely spoil the effect of the tint. Waxen sheets made in the above manner will not be either brittle in cold weather, nor too yielding in hot, nor are they much altered by time.

To save expense, it is always advisable to cut into sheets the blocks first made of white and other light color before any darker colors are made, because the scraps and spoiled sheets may then be melted again for the darker tints; for example, scraps of primrose wax will melt for a yellow or green; pink for a red; yellow for an orange; a light green to a darker tint; and so on. Also, in the after modelling of the flowers, the scraps are all valuable. If wax is frequently melted, it will require a little spirits of turpentine added to it.

We must now return to the white block cast, and show how it is to be cut into sheets. First, it is necessary to have a stop to fasten to the table the lump of wax; a piece of wood, three inches wide, and of which the following is a section, is well adapted for the purpose. (See cut next page.)

A, is the block of wax; B, the machine. The part C E rests on the table, to which it is held safely by the screw D; at C, is a cross piece of wood, which prevents the block of wax, represented as shaded in the cut, from slipping off. You must now get a carpenter's shave, called a spoke-shave (and those are of the best shape which are used by coopers). The wooden part which slides over the block of wax

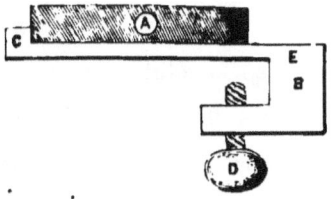

should be flat, and it should have rather a wide mouth or orifice where the iron passes. Grease well the iron and wooden under-face of the shave, and then force it along the wax, so as to cut off a thin slice, to make the surface even. This first slice will not be fit for use, nor yet perhaps the second or third. Soon, proceeding in the same manner, and keeping the tool well greased, slices or sheets will be cut off of equal and proper thickness. Such as are good must be kept for use, the rest re-melted.

A second method of cutting up the block, is to hold it in the hand, and force it along the greased surface of a larger wide-mouthed carpenter's plane.

A third method, which may be pursued by every

body without expense, is to have a number of pieces of writing paper cut rather smaller than the mould in which the wax has been cast. Take the block of wax out of the mould, and put into the mould as much paper as will just raise the block above the wired edge of the tin mould. Then fastening the mould, wax and all, firmly to a table, either by resting it on the stay before mentioned, or otherwise, as convenient; cut the top off even by a thin bladed dinner knife, taking care to run the knife steadily along the edge of the mould. Now take out the block, and put in a piece of paper to raise it up; put it in again, and you can cut off a sheet equal in thickness to the paper, the same operation repeated will give another slice; and so on, raising up the block by a piece of paper each time after a piece has been cut off. The only inconvenience here, is the removal of the block of wax each time from the casting mould; to prevent this, the stay which fixes to the table may have sides to it, when it is proposed to cut the wax by a knife, and it having no stop at one end of it, it can be taken out, and a piece of paper put beneath it with little trouble. If it be required to have long leaves, like those of a hyacinth, the mould to cast the wax in should be seven inches long, and one inch wide.

Colors required. — The ordinary colors used in painting flowers on paper, will also be required in imitating them in wax. The colors should all be transparent and bright; browns, blacks, and other dark colors are rarely ever wanted. For black we recollect only two uses, that of painting the anthers of the garden tulip, and to mix with carmine for the very dark rose, but even in this last case it is not necessary. The most useful colors are, — two shades of chrome yellow, smalt (powder blue), and Prussian blue; carmine, in powder, to color the wax, and afterwards, where necessary, to give a uniform tint to the petals. The following, in cakes, to be rubbed in the ordinary way of water colors, but with a little colorless ox gall, to make the colors lay upon the greasy surface of the wax: Cobalt, carmine, chrome, burnt sienna, sap green, Prussian blue, &c. These are to be laid on with the ordinary camel's hair pencils, and are adapted to make the ornamental marking of the flowers, such as the streaks of the tulip and carnation.

White and Green Down. — Some leaves and stalks have a certain degree of mealiness or hairiness about them, which it is desirable to imitate. For this purpose, sometimes a white, and at others a greenish white powder is used; any of those recommended for waxen fruit may be employed. Green flock is to be used for the hairiness of stems, and The mealiness or glaucous white color of the leaves of the carnation, pink, &c., may be made of hair powder, mixed with a little Brunswick or other green in a state of powder, they being rubbed together through a lawn or muslin sieve, to incorporate them well, and thus to make the color uniform.

Brushes.—The tinting-brush is for dry colors; the sizes and shapes are as follows:

Their use is to brush over the various shades of wax a different tint, where required; for example, the Eutoca Viscida is a flower of a beautiful blue color, but its centre is white, and the petals are lighter on their under side; therefore it must be made of white wax, and the blue color put on, before the petals are united together, by means of one of these brushes, and cobalt or ultramarine blue in powder. The cut shows the point of two different sized brushes.

Patterns and Shapes. — This is a very important matter, but presents no difficulty. The best of all patterns is the flower itself. Procure, if you can, two flowers like each other; one you are to keep perfect as a guide in making up, the second you may pull to pieces, which will enable you to count the number of the petals, to see their exact form, color, size, and shape. Take, then, one of each of the various parts, lay it upon a piece of white paper, and mark carefully round it with a pencil, so also of all the other parts. These are the guides, and in order that they may be available another time; you should write upon each the number required of them. The wax of proper color must then be selected, cut, colored, and moulded, according to these patterns. When flowers are readily procured, a selection should be made, and the patterns preserved for after use. Next to real flowers, the paintings of them of a natural size are of value, as it is easy, with a piece of tracing-paper, to take off any shape required, and afterwards to cut out a paper model according to its outline. Having mentioned a *paper* model, it may be stated that for making one flower only, a paper or card shape will do very well, but if a number are to be made, it is better to use thin tin. That called *tag-plate*, and which is used for the tags of laces, is the thinnest, and will cut very readily with scissors. At many places are sold pieces of tin for the purpose, but besides being very expensive, they are by no means correct, and imply that every individual leaf, bud, or floret made by them, must be exactly a counterpart to all the others; thus, a bunch of flowers, all exactly alike, as the May or White Thorn, the For-get-me-not, the Lilac, &c., would look extremely formal, however well they were arranged; though it is to be admitted, that these tin shapes very much diminish the labor of making such flowers as we have named, but to use them for Dahlias, Roses, &c., is unnecessary and unadvisable. The following shows these tin shapes for four flowers: 1 and

2, the For-get-me-not; 3, the Veronica; 4, the Lilac;

5, various shapes of the Dahlia, one within the other, forming a series of six sizes; 6, shape of the Primrose petal; 7, of the quilled China Aster, or made a little larger of the Chrysanthemum.

A circumstance here forces itself upon the attention, that, although the petal curves down to a point where it is united to the rest of the flowers, yet, when cutting out the shape, and afterwards the wax, this part is to be made wider than is natural, in order that it may adhere the stronger to the rest, and not be so liable to bend or snap afterwards; for all waxen flowers are apt to get a little brittle by time, particularly those that are made with wax, into which Canada balsam has been melted, as it is by some of the makers, greatly to its injury.

Stamens and Pointal. — The thread-like parts within flowers are made with white, yellow, or green cotton, made stiff first with starch, and then dipped in melted wax; this may be cut into lengths as required; bristles dyed of these colors are also useful; wax itself, cut into slips, will often be better than any thing else. The *seeds*, as they are called, sold at the artificial flower makers, are vile substitutes.

To make Waxen Leaves. — This is a method very different from making the petals of the flowers, although very often the petals, if made thus, would be very greatly improved. The waxen leaves are made partly by moulding, and partly by cutting; but as they are made of sheets of wax previously prepared, the method of making them properly belongs to this department of the subject. First, take the natural leaf, and make a pattern of it in tin or card, with all its irregularities of outline, place it upon wet sand, and pour plaster of Paris over it to the thickness of half an inch. When set, trim it round; turn it over, and cast in like manner the other side, but without disturbing the leaf itself. Separate the parts when the last plaster is set, take out the leaf, and you will have two moulds of it, which are ready for use immediately, and will, if carefully used, last for a long time. To make the leaves themselves of wax, take a sheet of the latter, cut it by the tin pattern into proper size, soak the mould in water just warm, and while thus wet and warm, squeeze the waxen shape between the two half moulds; they will impress upon it all the various veins and irregularities of the real leaf. The most usual leaves made are those of the Hyacinth, the Camellia, Rose, Orange, Geranium, Convolvulus, Passion Flower, Hop, Laburnum, Primrose, Violet, and Water Lily. Some flowers never have leaves attached to them, as the Dahlia, Anemone, Ranunculus, Poppy, &c. The leaves, in these examples, are much divided, and would be very difficult to imitate; nor are they necessary, as they are never found in nosegays containing these flowers.

To make Succulent Stems, Buds, &c. — Many objects, which may be considered as accessories to flowers, require to be cast exactly in the manner already described under waxen fruit. There are various succulent Stems, as those of the cactus, stapelia, aloe, &c.; the Buds of the larger fuchsias, berries of coffee, very small oranges, buds of the dahlia, hips of the rose tree, &c., yet casting is to be avoided as much as possible, on account of the trouble of it, and the too great uniformity of the produce; generally the buds of flowers may be modelled very well by the hand, without having recourse to the inconveniences of casting; the latter process being chiefly of use to those who make the commoner kind of waxen flowers for sale.

MODELLING SIMPLE FLOWERS.

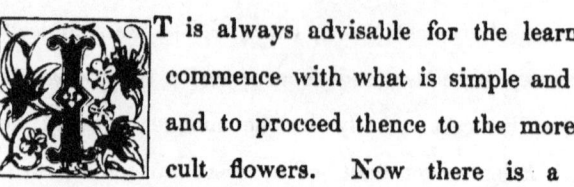

IT is always advisable for the learner to commence with what is simple and easy, and to proceed thence to the more difficult flowers. Now there is a great trouble in producing a fac-simile of personate flowers like the Foxglove, and all those flowers which are bell or trumpet-shaped,—as the Blue Bell, the Convolvulus, Tobacco, the Marvel of Peru, and others; still greater difficulty would be found with many of the Orchideous plants, the Calceolaria, &c., while others are so remarkably easy, that even a first attempt generally succeeds in producing a good imitation; such, for example, are the Primrose, the Heart's Ease, the Laburnum, the Pink, &c. We shall describe many of these beautiful objects in detail, only observing, that with all flowers it is advisable first to cut out and arrange all the pieces required; then to color them properly, afterwards to attach the parts to each other, and finally to put on such extra touches of colors, down, varnish, &c., as they seem to require.

A little knowledge of botany will greatly assist, because it teaches the character of the flower in its single natural state, showing the number of its leaves, or, more properly, petals, and the number of the stamens or inner thread-like bodies, and also the various positions of these and other parts relatively to each other. All flowers of the same species, and generally of the same family, are like each other in these and other respects; thus, although there are twenty or more species of Crocus, and of these perhaps fifty varieties, yet they all agree in having six parts to the flower, three outside the other three, with three stamens within side, and a pointal in the centre of all. By knowing, then, the character of one Crocus, we know the character of all, and require no form or pattern but a single petal; our botanical knowledge supplying all other information. Lest we should not be understood by the non-botanist, through being too scientific in speaking of the parts of a flower, we have to state, that the outer envelope of a flower is called a calyx, and its parts are called sepals; this is generally a green cup, as in the Primrose, yet sometimes colored, as in the Fuchsia; and when a flower has but one kind of envelope, as the Crocus and the Tulip, it is a calyx. When the flower has two envelopes, the inner part is a corolla, and its parts are called petals, as the red leaves or petals of the Rose. Sometimes the calyx falls off when the flower opens, as the Poppy. Within the corolla are the stamens or threads, and in the centre of all the pointal, and sometimes the young seed-vessel.

SINGLE AND SIMPLE FLOWERS.

THE SNOWDROP, CROCUS, PRIMROSE, AND VIOLET.

RIMROSE. The character of all the tribe is to have the calyx in one piece, with five feet on the top. The corolla of one piece, five-cleft at the top, five stamens, and one pointal.

Choose the palest colored yellow wax, one sheet will be enough for two flowers and two buds; also, bright green wax for the calyx and leaves, — one sheet will make two leaves or four buds. Cut the calyx, as shown at A; and five petals, as at B. Paint each petal with a spot in the middle, as shown, with a dark orange yellow. Choose a piece of moderately thick wire for a stalk, three or four inches long, cover it with a slip of green wax, and make a little knob at the point. Then take a piece of yellow wax, half an inch long, and a quarter of an inch wide; cut this with the scissors into five strips for stamens, stick these on the top of the wire, or rather on the knob which terminates it, then put on in like manner the five petals; afterwards, take the calyx in a warm palm of the hand, roll over it the knob of one of the curling pins, so that it may gradually curl up, that the edges may be joined together, assisting this curling up by folding them with the fingers. When thus made warm and pliant, fold it carefully over a small pencil or round stick, made wet, until the edges slightly lap over each other, rub down these edges so that they

---

In cutting out the patterns, always lay them lengthwise of the sheet of wax, as it is much less brittle cut thus, than if the petals were cut crosswise. It is advisable also, in cold weather, to warm the wax a little, before it is cut up.

unite neatly. Thrust the wire part of the pin down within the calyx and between that and the centre stick, in five places, corresponding to the top of the teeth. This, if carefully done, will form the calyx into five ribs, as in nature, and as shown in section in the cut; or it may be improved in this respect by having a pentagonal stick instead of a round one, or it may be finished when removed from the stick. When made, pass the calyx up from the bottom end of the stalk. Fasten it in the proper place, so that its points shall come under the corolla, and fix it by pinching its lower end with the stalk. Lastly, make the flower of proper form, by bending all the petals quite flat, not individually, for each may have a little folding or other irregularity given to it, but merely that the whole flower shall be flat and not cup-shaped.

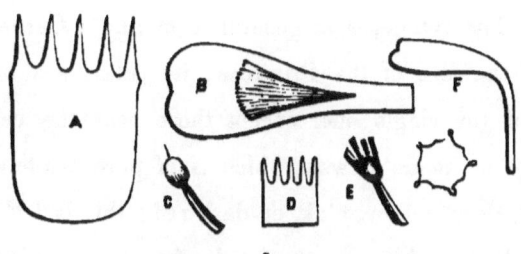

The corolla of the Primrose is in nature but of one piece, formed at the lower part like a tube, and spread out in the upper part into five parts, but it is much more difficult to make it so in wax; nor is the effect, when made, better than when made in five pieces.

To form the bud, take one or two yellow petals only, curl them round, and nearly bury them in the calyx. The leaf, to be natural, must be cast in a proper mould; and should, when made, be dusted underneath with the white down.

The Common Primrose — "that pale visitant of balmy Spring," as Bidlake calls it — is not always so pale; for when cultivated, it not only becomes double, but sports into white and various colors. The double variety may be made white, sulphur colored, pale pink, and dark red; the form of a double Primrose is shown in the cut on page 72. When thus double, the peculiar dark spot painted on the single variety is not found, but the whole flower is of a uniform tint. The whole flower thus double, is in general form like a Carnation, but of the size of the Primrose; its petals are of the form of the single one, except those near the centre. It may be made of wax which is of pure white, pale yellow, deep yellow, pink, or dark red; this last should be made by white wax painted with dry carmine by the tinting brush, before it is cut out, and the cut edges touched with the same after cutting.

Other flowers of the primrose tribe are the Cowslip, the Polyanthus, the Auricula, the Chinese Primrose; all these have many flowers upon the same stem, and all coming out of the top of it. The cowslip has cup-shaped flowers, the others have their flowers flat like the primrose; the cowslip is smaller than the primrose, and darker, with a still darker spot upon each division of the corolla. The manner of making the primrose will suggest the modelling of the others. The polyanthus is to be made of bright yellow wax; the auricula generally of white wax; the mealiness of this last may be put on best thus: Damp the parts which are to be mealy with turpentine, and dust arrow-root or hair-powder over them; the leaves are of a dark bluish green; they must also be dusted with white.

The Crocus Tribe. — All Crocuses have six petals, or rather sepals, colored alike, and formed into a long tube below; three of the sepals are rather within the other three. There are three stamens and one pointal. Choose first the common yellow crocus, which is seen expanded on page 72. Cut the sepals and stamens of the size and form shown at A and B; the former of gold-colored wax, either cast of proper color, or yellow wax to which a more golden hue is given by deep chrome, or rather of deep orange. When the stamens are formed, damp them with turpentine, and dip them, while damp, into powdered dark chrome. Form the pointal, as represented at C, of yellow wax on the end of a wire, damp it with turpentine, and dip it into powdered carmine, with a little orange mixed, or not to spoil the carmine by mixing another color with it, this last may be dusted over afterwards. Join the three stamens to three of the sepals, first having rolled them in the hand with the ball end of the pin, so that each sepal may be somewhat boat-shaped. The lower end of the stamens should blend with the sepal to which it is attached, so that their union is not observed. The point of union should also be below the expanded part of the flower. Put a little bit of spare wax around the base of the pointal, and fasten the sepals to it by pressure, first putting on the three which bear the stamens at equal distances, and then the other three. Unite them, if possible, so as to form a tube at the base, and spread them out somewhat at the top, according as an open or closed flower is desired; sheaths or large folding leaves of light brown wax may be placed over the stem, first one on one side, then one on the contrary. Between the lowest sheath and the stem may be placed the leaves. When a crocus is in flower, the leaves generally have not grown so tall as the flower, they must be always cut out of dark green wax, and have a white stripe painted up the centre of each.

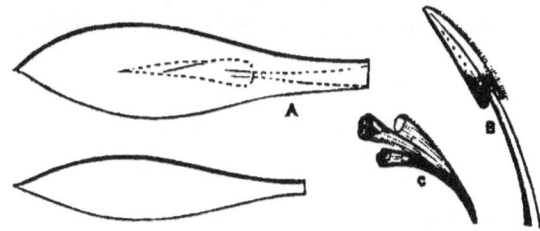

The cut on page 72, also shows a bud of the Scotch Crocus; this species is yellow, with brown pencilling on the outside of the sepals; it has always two flowers to a root.

Crocus Sativus, or the Saffron Crocus, shown in the cut, blossoms in the autumn; it is a fine purple, with yellow stigma and stamens. The pretty little Cloth-of-gold Crocus is a bright yellow, marked outside with brown, and its sepals are turned downwards, when the flower is full out.

The Colchicum is to be modelled in the same way as the crocus. It is of a purplish pink color, and has six stamens; also, the Sternbergia, a bright-yellow autumn flower, of the size and form of the crocus, but with six stamens. Numerous other flowers will suggest themselves as of the same character.

The Snowdrop.—Take a wire of small size, about six inches long. Next a piece of white wax, a quarter of an inch square, and cut this into six thread-like strips, after the manner of a fringe. Twist this around the end of the wire, so that the six points hang down a little way. You need not be particular about this, because, as the flower always hangs down, the centre part is not much seen. Then cut three of each of the two patterns given of pure white wax; make each of them hollow, rubbing them by the ball while warmed by the hand. Then put on at equal distance the three inner petals, so that they adhere well to the stalk, and completely cover the stamens, and also that they overlap each other a little. Next, put on the three outer petals. Paint the inner ones with a spot of bright green, made of a mixture of Prussian blue and chrome yellow, and laid on with a camel's hair or sable brush of small size. At the foot of the flower put a little piece of green wax to form a small ball; bend the stalk, and add to it, distant from the flower, a sheath made of very thin green wax; when there are to be leaves shown, there should be always two on the stalk; but when a pot full of Snowdrops is to be represented, there may be many leaves arising from the ground without a flower at all; observe in this case, also, there should be always two together. Snowdrops should always be shown two or three together.

The Violet. — This simple flower, which is of five petals, may be made of blue sheet wax, of the proper color at first, or white wax, colored either with oil or dry colors, after being cut into petals; the latter is to be preferred, because it gives a finer tint. Sometimes White Violets are made; their form is the same as the dark purple ones. It is the botanical characteristic of the Sweet-scented Violet, that its flowers grow on stalks which come at once from the root of the plant, as also the leaves; thus the plant is never branched, and, properly speaking, there is no real stem to it; although each leaf and flower has its distinct stalk. Owing to this, it is very easy to make, and looks well when in an imitation garden-pot, or in a bunch of two or three together. There is a calyx of one piece, which however is five pointed, the points not very sharp.

A, calyx, to be cut rather larger than the pattern. B, shape of lower petal. C, side petal. D, top petal.

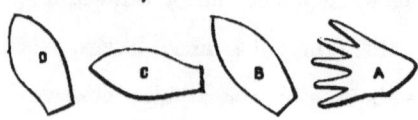

First, form the centre of the flower of a small piece of dark yellow wax; this is to be scarcely larger than the wire which forms the stalk; indeed, it is but the piece of wax folded over the stalk, and pointed up at the end. It may be snipped with scissors after being put on, to resemble five stamens closely packed together. Now put on the five petals, — one below, one at each side, and two at the top. All the petals are considerably hollowed in the hand first, particularly the three lower ones. When these are fixed, wrap the calyx around the purple petals, so that each point of it comes to the interval between the petals; or, in other words, so that the points are seen from the face of the flower; the upper part of the stalk end of the flower should be rather fuller than the lower, as if the stalk came out in some degree from the bottom, as well as the end of the flower. The calyx and leaves are of a bright green.

The Heartsease. — The whole of the Heartsease are of the tribe of the violet, and therefore consist of the same parts, and are equally as easy to imitate, except, that many of them require much after-coloring. The Heartsease has very rarely any scent, and it is branched; that is, although each flower has its own foot stalk, yet there are many flowers and leaves to the same stem; the leaves, too, are very different from those of the violet. The flowers are of every variety of purple, blue, yellow, white, and occasionally brown color; but never red. They are also of every size, from the wild one of the fields, which is scarcely half an inch across, to the splendid productions of the garden, eight inches or more in circumference.

THE TULIP, HYACINTH, AND NARCISSUS.

The Tulip is not an easy flower to make, although so apparently simple. This simplicity, indeed, constitutes half the difficulty, as the flower, when formed, is so large as to show all defects, and is not relieved by leaves, tendrils, or any other adjunct which can hide a misshapen petal, &c. In fact, a Tulip, to be a beautiful object in wax, must be made with perfect exactness. Tulips vary very much in their color, shape, and mode of streaking; some have yellow bodies, and others white; some black anthers, others yellow; and so accordant with each other must be the anthers, streaks, color, size, and form, that only a real Tulip must be taken as a pattern. Upon the examination of this, it will be found that the young seed-vessel is found of a club-shape in the centre; next, are six stamens at equal distances; next, six petals; the whole supported on a strong stem. The petals should be made of white wax for white flowers, and a middle shade of yellow for the other varieties. The color for the streaks is a mixture of carmine with a little blue or black, using Prussian blue to produce a purple; and Indian ink, with the carmine or lake, to form a deep crimson. Great care must be taken in laying on the streaks, as these must be on both sides of the petal, and before this is attached to the stalk: also, each petal is to be rolled with the knob of the largest curling pin, until it is somewhat of a boat shape, or much hollowed in the part that is to come next the stalk. Three of the petals are to be put on first, and the other three afterwards in such a manner, that their edges will somewhat overlap the edges of the others; the whole flower, if fully blown, will form a cup-shape; but it is far more elegant to contract the top much more than this, so as to show fully the outside of the petals.

The Van Trol, or Sweet-scented Early Spring Tulip, is very easy to make. Its petals are about an inch and a half long, and three quarters or less in width, round below and pointed above. They are to be made of deep yellow wax, and colored all over with carmine, except around the edges, which are to be left yellow. When put together, the petals are seldom regular, but somewhat distorted, so as to appear twisted towards the top an effect easily imitated; the flower should also be represented as nearly closed.

In wax, these small Tulips are usually represented as growing in a garden-pot; there are to be two leaves for each; if thus made, never put more than three in a pot.

The Hyacinth. — This beautiful production of the garden is of every possible color, except bright green, scarlet, brown, and black; its varieties, both single and double, running through every shade of blue, pink, yellow, white, &c. It is rarely or never streaked, but very often the centre of a double flower is of a much darker color than the outer petals. The form of the Hyacinth is different from any former flower we have described, inasmuch as it consists of numberless florets, united together to form a close bunch. This adds somewhat to the labor, but not the difficulty of manipulation. First, cut from twelve to twenty pieces of thin wire, eight inches long; then cut out the petals according to form A. If you are imitating a single flower, take a piece of white wax, a quarter of an inch broad, and half an inch long, cut this in narrow strips, roll a piece similar to this round the top of each wire, one end of each strip being attached to the wire, the other end beyond it, these are for stamens; if you wish a double flower, let there be either six or twelve of these, or rather of narrow petals as a substitute for the stamens; those for the inner row are to be of form B; and for the second row of form C; being a gradation in size from the outer or true petals, which are also six in number. The various petals, when cut out, will require after-coloring or not, according to the variety copied. The stamens being attached, next fix the six petals at equal distances around, smooth very carefully the joints of them near to the stalk, so that they shall appear united for nearly half their length. Let the petals remain quite close together at the top for the buds, a little more open for the next lowest flowers, and the petals of the full-blown ones, quite curved back in a round and regular form, for this character is very essential to the Hyacinth. If a double flower is to be imitated, first, instead of the stamens, fix the six inner petals;

then, in the intervals of these, the next row; and in the intervals between these last, or exactly opposite the inner row, the largest petals; the base of all the under ones is covered with the upper row, and the whole base is nicely rounded off. The petals are then put into form, by carefully bending back first the outer row, then the next, and lastly the inner ones. One or even both rows of inner petals may be dispensed with for the buds, particularly the smaller ones. The joining of the florets together is the same for single and double flowers. The following brief instruction may suffice for many other flowers besides the Hyacinth: Provide a needleful of green silk, and cover each stalk for about an inch with green wax. Arrange the bud and flower in the order of their degree of expansion; fasten two of the smallest together, half an inch from the floret, by a curl of the silk; a quarter of an inch lower down, fasten on a third floret or bud, by another turn of the silk, and so on for about three or four inches down the stems, increasing the distance of a quarter of an inch for each as you proceed downwards, and also rather increasing the half inch distance from the floret to the place of the ligature; after placing two or three, it will be necessary to bend the stem of the floret sideways. It will be observed, in a natural flower, the buds are upright; the fresh-blown florets, horizontal to the stem; and the lower one, rather hanging down. As you go on attaching these florets, the stem will need covering with a strip of green wax, similar to that used at first. Doing this with care, nicely blending the edges of these pieces, and duly arranging the florets so as to touch each other all round, a very natural appearance will be given to the whole; and should a Hyacinth be even the very first flower to be imitated, the learner will generally have cause to congratulate herself upon her successful modelling. For a fine Hyacinth, you will not require more than four sheets of wax, as it cuts to great advantage.

The Narcissus. — The name Narciss or Narcissus, is rather that of a family than a particular flower, as the species are extremely numerous, and general among us. Space only allows one to be fully described; but the instructions given for that apply to them all, especially if the following remarks relative to the peculiarities of each are borne in mind.

Jonquil (*Narcissus Jonquillus*). — This is wholly, cup and all, of a bright yellow, the stems are thin and long; there are two sheaths. The flower is about two inches across, and there are two or three to each stem. The leaves are short and narrow.

Poet's Narciss (*Narcissus poeticus*). — There is but a single flower to each stem, and this is very often double, of a pure white color; when single, the cup is white tipped with scarlet. The seed-vessel is very small, the stem rather slender.

Polyanthus Narciss (*Narcissus Tageta*). — Eight or ten flowers to a stalk, of a fine dark yellow color, both as to petals and cup; the latter, however, is much the darker, and may be made of orange wax, while the petals are of the darkest shade of yellow. The flowers need not be more than an inch and a half over, or even less than this.

Two-flowered Narciss (*Narcissus biflorus.*) — This two-flowered species is one of the prettiest, and as easy as any other to imitate, we will therefore describe it more in detail than the rest. The petals are, as in every case of the others, six in number; the stamens six; the nectary or centre part in the form of a cup. This is of a yellow color, jagged around the edge. The petals are white; the sheath of a light brown; and the stem and leaves bright green. First, take two moderately thick wires for the stem, and cover two or three inches of the top of each with green wax. Model six stamens of the form given in the illustrative cut. Dip the points of these in turpentine; and then, while wet, in dry orange chrome. Lay them aside for the turpentine to evaporate, and for them to become hard again. While the stamens are drying, cut out a piece of deep yellow wax, of the form shown at A, and make it jagged around the edge. Hold this piece in the hand, and roll the ball of the curling pin over it backwards and forwards, till it curls up, and till the edges may be brought together. You may then unite the edges,

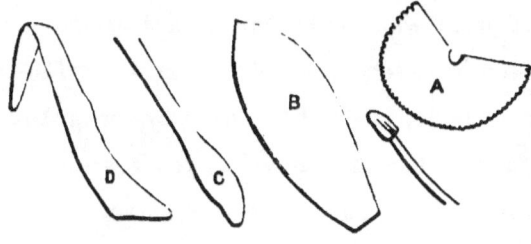

and still roll it with the pin, till it forms a perfect regular cup. The petals will not require rolling; but if you have a natural flower to copy from, you will find that the natural ones are somewhat in ridges, this effect is produced by the pin being pressed against them lengthways. Unite the six stamens to the wire stem, so that they shall just have their anthers projecting beyond it. Next pierce the centre of the cup by the bottom end of the stalk, and pass it up to its proper place; that is, so that the bottom of it comes up close to the anthers of the stamens, which have just been put on; pinch this tightly on. Place the petals at regular intervals under the cup, bending them across at about a quarter of an inch near the bottom, and putting them on by this quarter of an inch, which will be quite sufficient. Wrap a piece of white wax, for about an inch, along the wire for the tube of the flower, and make the whole quite smooth and even; lastly, finish the flower with a little oblong ball of green wax of the same color as the stem, to form the seed-vessel, as shown at C. The other flower is to be made the same way, or a bud may be formed in like manner. The petals are to be bent so as to give the flower a flat appearance; or rather, a flower opening is to be somewhat hollow; in a full-blown flower, the petals are to be flat, and in one which has been open for two or three days; they are to be bent back. The two flowers are now to be tied together at about an inch and a half from the seed-vessel of the one, and an inch from the seed-vessel of the other. Tie them not only here, but downwards along the stem to the bottom of it with thin soft cotton or silk. Cut out of brown wax a sheath, shaped as D, join it to the stem so as to conceal the upper ligature, and cover the stem below the sheath with green wax. The flowers only remain to be bent into proper form, so as to arrange themselves gracefully. They are naturally bent immediately adjoining the seed-vessel or bulb, at the bottom of the tube of the flower.

THE PINK, JESSAMINE, DAISY, FORGET-ME-NOT, COREOPSIS, AND CYCLAMEN.

The Pink, Carnation, Clove, &c. — Many of the Pinks are beautiful objects for modelling, and by no means difficult, whether single or double. We will begin with the single Indian Pink, as shown in the centre of the above illustration. This flower is an annual, of a fine scarlet color, with black markings upon it as represented. First, take a moderately-thick wire, fix upon the end of this the pointal, which is of a forked character in all Pinks, Cloves, &c., as shown more fully at C, in the succeeding cut. Next color a sheet of white wax of a deep crimson with carmine on both sides of it, but rather paler on the underside. Then cut out five petals, with long points, nearly of the shape shown at B, but rather fuller in the body, and with a different edge, as seen above. Put the proper markings on each petal with black, not too regularly, for fear of stiffness in appearance. Place the five petals around the top of the stalk, and bend each back, when put on; and it is advisable in this, and many other cases, where the petals or other parts are to have a sudden bend given to them, to warm them for a moment in the sun or before a fire, to prevent the wax from snapping across; it is particularly necessary in petals, which, like those of the Pink, have a long, narrow end to them; this part being necessarily weak, and liable to accident. Form a calyx of bright green wax, of the shape of A, beneath, but smaller; roll it into a tube, with a closed end, as before described for the Primrose; bring it up to the flower from the bottom of the stalk, unite it well, and the flower is finished; except that there are two or three small leaves or bracts, as they are called, at the base of the calyx.

The Single Pink is made in precisely the same manner as the Indian Pink last described, but rather larger. The petals are of white wax, colored towards the end of the body of them with a fine purple, made of lake and Prussian blue, laid on with a camel's hair or sable pencil. The wax which forms the calyx must be of a dark green, powdered over, when the flower is finished, with arrow-root or other white downy powder, to give the slight degree of mealiness observed on this flower, as well as upon the Clove, Carnation, &c.

The Double Pink contains from thirty to forty petals, all of the same shape, except that the inner ones are somewhat narrower than those near the edge. The petals being ready, attach them around the top of the stem, folding each more or less back, till the whole together shall form a shape similar to about one third of an orange cut off. There are great varieties of pinks, the markings, edgings, and form of which vary considerably.

Clove and Carnation. — We somewhat forestall the subject of double flowers, by introducing here the Double Clove, the Carnation, and Picatee. The formation of them is the same as for a double pink. The cut on page 96 shows the shape of the various parts at A, E, and D; while F shows the general shape of the flower when complete. E is a full sized petal of a Carnation, with the markings or stripes required; but these flowers, as well as the Picatees, are so extremely varied in these respects, that, as in the case of the Tulip, Ranuculus, and others, a real flower, or a good colored copy of one, must be had as a pattern. They may all be made

of white wax, colored as circumstances require; some Picatees may be made of light yellow, and cloves of pink wax, colored with dry lake, or carmine mixed with a little black, to give the peculiar dark crimson of the Clove. The markings of the Carnation are generally of carmine for some of the stripes, and of a purple for others.

The Jasmine. — Choose the finest wire for the stalk, the darkest green for the leaves, and the purest white wax for the flower. The cut on page 93 will show the general arrangement and shape of the various parts; the flowers are there represented as of full size, but the leaf is in nature about double of that depicted. No particular remark is to be made relative to the formation of the flower itself; all is extremely easy, the only care is to join the two edges of the tube of the white flower carefully, for it may be made all in one piece. To bend this part, and all other tubular flowers, fold the wax, while warm, over the stem of the curling pin, or of a wire of proper size. In this flower there are no stamens required to be seen.

The Daisy. — For the centre of a Daisy, cut a strip of deep yellow wax, an inch or more in length, and a quarter of an inch broad, into thread-like strips; not quite, however, cutting through the whole width, thus not quite separating each from the others; twist the piece thus cut round the end of a wire, and trim the tops of them, so as altogether to be of a round form. This ought now to resemble the top of a round painting brush, about a quarter of an inch over; trim them up at the back also, so as not to cut them separate from each other, lest they fall apart, but merely to make them smooth and even; next take a round piece of white wax, and cut it into from twenty to thirty divisions, as shown in the representation of the Daisy flower on page 93, pass this up from the bottom of the stalk, and press it until it adheres well around the centre boss. Next cut a circular piece of green wax half the size of the white piece, and join it beneath. The flower will thus be formed.

The Forget-me-not. — This is a very different flower from any we have yet attempted. It had better be cut from white wax by a tin shape, of which one is given of proper form on page 65. Color them of a bright blue, except near the very centre of the flower, where it should be of a pure white, while the five thread-like stamens are of a bright yellow. The flower buds are pink. The flowers may be scattered, or in a close spike, as they are found of both characters. The stem must be of fine wire, the flowers and buds formed separately, and put on so that the most pinkish ones are at the top of the bunch; these are very small, and are curled round, like a scorpion's tail. The blue used to color the wax for the florets should be cobalt or ultramarine, the former is the best. Two or three bunches of flowers may be upon the same stem.

The Coreopsis. — The light delicate character of this

flower, and its rich color, give great effect to a group. It is to be made precisely in the same manner as the Daisy; the centre is black, slightly sprinkled with yellow, the petals are a deep rich orange, and the marks upon them are a rich brown, formed by burnt umber painted upon them. The calyx is light green, and formed of a number of small leaves placed lapping over each other. There are nine or ten petals, and they are jagged at the edge, as shown in the flower at the right of the cut on page 93.

The Cyclamen. — This is the next flower in order, and is represented on page 93. It differs from all the others in having the petals, which are five in number, bent back. The flowers are altogether curious. They are of a whitish pink color in the English species, and to be formed of white wax, slightly tinted with carmine or lake. The stamens are not visible, therefore they need not be made. The stalk is about three inches long, and it is to have a small lump of wax at the end of it, to form the flower upon; the petals are to be held to the fire for a moment to be made very pliable, then placed on the little lump and pressed down tight; each one as it is put on being turned up, as shown in the cut. The calyx and stalk are to be of very dark green wax. The calyx is of one piece cut at the rim into five blunt points. The seed-vessel is of a light brown; it may be made of any refuse pieces, and is about the size of a small pea, but oval; its calyx half covers it. The leaves are of a very dark green, with white lines and margin. Each flower and leaf grows on a separate stalk, which rises immediately from the root. The stem of the seed-vessel is curiously twisted round and round, like a corkscrew, and more so as the seed ripens, until at length the seed-vessel lies on the ground, and thus it may be said to sow its own seed.

Another species of variety of Cyclamen is common in the gardens or green-houses, the petals of which are beautifully tinted with a fine dark pink, near the lower end of them, or for about a quarter of an inch of the part turned over. The leaves are the same. There is also the Cyclamen Coum, with small short scarlet flowers and round or kidney-shaped leaves.

OTHER SIMPLE FLOWERS.

The manner of making the above flowers will show the general management to be observed with all flowers of a simple character; to imitate them with facility requires only a little practice; and presuming that the tyro has already attained some little degree of facility of operation, it will not be necessary to enter into others with so minute particulars: the following remarks may, however, be useful, and, with a real flower to work with, no difficulty can arise. The flowers which are next enumerated, are such as can be made in wax with much perfection, and are such as are usually chosen for that purpose.

The Laburnum. — This is one of the prettiest and easiest flowers to make in wax. Twelve or fourteen flowers or buds may form the bunch. They are to be of the brightest yellow wax, and made on slender wire. The flower consists of a crooked lump for the bottom, then two side pieces, and a standard at top; this last has several veins of dark purple upon its inner side. The whole, when finished, will be drooping, and therefore in much estimation to group with more stiff and massive flowers.

The Convolvulus. — A very difficult flower. The varieties white, with five pink stripes; or purple with pink stripes are the prettiest. After having cut the shapes all of one color, — that is, either white left uncolored, or tinted on the inner side with fine rich blue, with a trace of red in it, — lay upon the piece thus cut, to form the flower, five long triangular strips of pink wax; rub them gently, till they adhere nicely; then, having it warm, fold it over the wooden forming shape (Convolvulus moulding stick); being careful to soak the shape for a minute or two in warm, but not hot water; first rub it gently on the outside, until the edges come together, when they must be joined very carefully and neatly. Form the rim in proper shape, according to the flower copied, and take it off the mould. Now prepare the stem, which may be a rather thick wire; finer wires, ready waxed, being used for the flowers and leaves. There is always a flower on one side the stalk, and a leaf opposite to it on the other, a circumstance very likely to be overlooked. The buds come out very rapidly, and the flowers decay as soon; thus, in a group there should never be more than one or two flowers expanded. The bud is twisted before opening. The leaf is heart-shaped.

The Fuchsia. — Every year brings us new species of Fuchsia, some small and with solitary flowers, others tubular and with flowers in bunches; the former are by much the easier to imitate. The leaves are in pairs, of a middle shade of green, veined with purple or scarlet. From the junction of each leaf with the stem arises a flower, which must be joined at once to the stem; the flower stems of fine copper wire, that they may be weak and pendulous. All the wire used must be waxed, by rubbing it over with a piece of wax, in the same manner as a thread is waxed by the tailor. Have the leaves of different sizes, and the smaller of a lighter color than the others. Join two opposite each other on the end of the stem, then two others near to them on the opposite sides of the stem at a little distance down, two others in the same position as the top pair. Out of the axillæ of these, and indeed of the last pair also, may be seen little buds, with stalks of half an inch long, next an inch, and a little pendulous, then of an inch and a half, progressing to two or more inches, when full-blown flowers will be seen. In placing them on, first tie on the flowers, then put the leaves over the joints where these were attached. The flowers are made thus: They have eight stamens, four inner petals of a fine purple color, and, lastly, a scarlet calyx, somewhat tubular, and with four points like petals. The fine wire itself, colored pink towards the points, forms a pointal in the centre, which extends down an inch from the flower; a minute ball is at the end of it, made by just dipping the end in melted wax. Next follow eight scarlet stamens, which extend down half an inch, then comes the purple corolla, and finally the scarlet calyx. This last entirely hides the corolla when the flower is closed. The berry is dark purple, and of an oval shape. A beautiful variety, which looks well in wax, called Victoria victrix, has the calyx of a pure white, and the corolla a dark purple. Of the larger Fuchsias, the buds are generally cast in a mould in the same manner as for waxen fruit. The following is an engraving of a large Fuchsia, in which every part is of the natural size.

WAX FLOWERS.

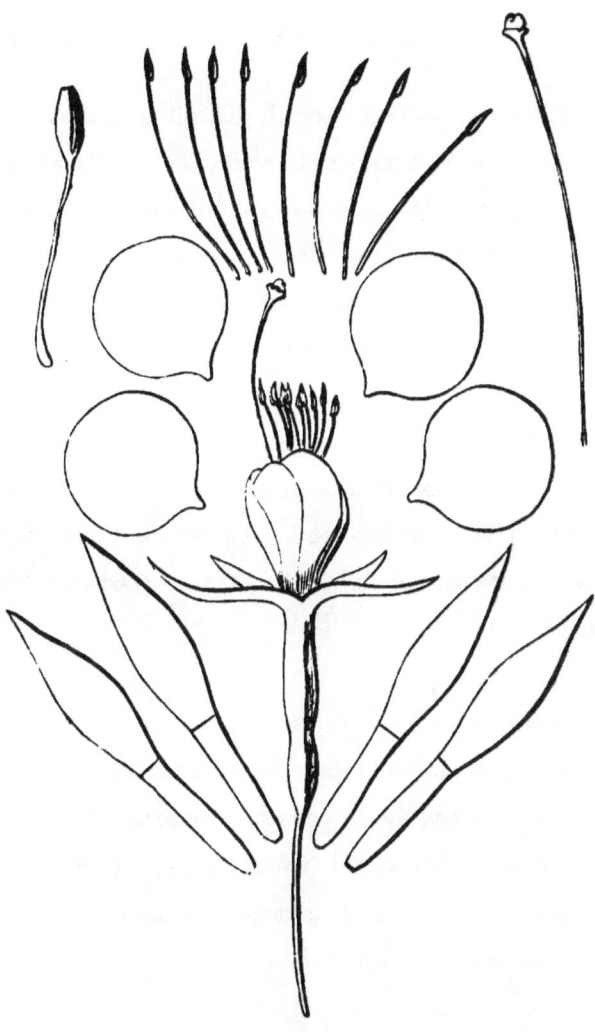

Various parts of the Fuchsia of the natural size, being drawn from an actual flower.

Bell Flowers. — These are all difficult to make; they are most of a blue or purple color, the corolla of one piece, and its edge cut into five divisions or teeth. They may be bent into shape upon a proper moulding stick made on purpose, according to the size and the shape of the flower to be imitated.

The Tobacco. — The noblest species, the Virginian Tobacco, is made in the same manner as the bell flowers; it is of a fine pink, and tubular; the calyx is also somewhat tubular. It is a very good object in wax.

Honeysuckle. — This is a trumpet-shaped or tubular flower, made of yellow wax, somewhat stained with red. It has five prominent stamens. It may be made readily with a real flower to copy from. The Wild Honeysuckle looks perhaps the best if it is of white wax shaded with pink.

The Poppy. — This flower is difficult to make, and the only kind that should be attempted is the Scarlet or Field Poppy. First, procure a wire of moderate thickness, and cover it with green worsted; at the top end place an oval lump of green wax, which you are to cut transversely, so that the top shall be nearly flat, and of the full size of the lump of wax; make upon this several lines or marks from the centre outwards, also a little irregularity around the edge, from line to line. Cut a strip of dark purple wax into stamens of a thread-like form, without separating the one from the other. Dip the outer ends in gum water, and then into a black or purple powder, to represent the anthers. Place these close all around and underneath the seed-vessel, pressing them down tight and firm, so as to surround it with very numerous stamens. Then take the thinnest sheets of wax you can get, cut four petals of proper form, and paint them with vermilion on both sides; crumple these gently up in the hand, and then opening them carefully, press the ends of them under the stamens, putting on first those on two opposite sides, and afterwards the other two to fold over them. No leaves are wanted; it is better to have the flower drooping.

The Passion Flower.—This is rather a difficult subject to make; but no one looks more natural, or more beautiful when complete, with its flowers, tendrils, leaves, and somewhat climbing stem; it climbs.

however, not by any convolution of the stem itself, as does the Convolvulus, but by the tendrils which the young stem throws out to support its growth upwards. No description can give an idea of the flower itself; the centre of it is a curiously-formed column, with three spreading, club-shaped arms upon the top of it. This must all be modelled of green wax, a wire running up the centre. Out of the lower part of the central column grow five stamens, the anthers of these must be modelled of dark yellow wax, except their filaments, which may be of fine green wire waxed. A fine bright blue ring of filaments, like rays, are seated around the lower part, and this is supported by ten, or sometimes twelve, white petals, each of them is a little hollowed, and every other one throughout is somewhat larger than the intermediate ones, and a little hooked at the end; the back of these petals is generally a little green. The tendrils are made of a thin green wire, made by twisting it round a pencil, then pulling it out loosely. The leaves are a very dark green, which may be made of wax and stamped, or they may be bought ready made. The Passion Flower should always be made along with its stem, &c., and hung gracefully over a vase. There is a very fine species of Passion Flower, often beautifully modelled. 'It is of a fine crimson color, with the rays partly colored with a darker tint.

The Single Rose. — The Single is much more difficult to model than the Double one, yet the Sweetbrier and the Wild Rose would look unnatural if doubled. First, cut a number of stamens, and tip them with knobs of yellow. Place these in a loose bunch around the end of the stem wire, rather spreading them out from the centre, but not formally or stiffly. Cut five heart-shaped petals of white wax, color them of a pinkish hue with carmine, and place them at equal distances around and under the stamens. Next, cut five irregular green leaves, which place underneath them, for a calyx. Lastly, form of green wax a perfectly smooth, longish, oval ball, which pass the wire through at the bottom, and bring it up close to the calyx, which must be very smoothly and evenly joined to it. The leaves are of five leaflets of different sizes. The rosebud is of a pointed oval form; the calyx leaves inclosing all, or nearly all, of the petals, more or less, according to its expansion. A small oval seed-vessel is seen beneath the bud.

The Chrysanthemum, China Aster, and other quilled

WAX FLOWERS.

Flowers. — These are different from those before described. They are not, properly speaking, double flowers, but are of that character called compound flowers, the nature of which is, that it consists of a great number of flowers upon one receptacle or base, the corolla of each is tubular, and being increased much in size by cultivation, the whole has a very compound or doubled appearance. The best way of making these quilled flowers is this: Procure a tin shape, such as that given in No. 7, on page 65. Stamp two or three hundred pieces of white, pink, or purple wax, of the color of the intended flower, and as many pieces of thin wire covered with silk, these last half an inch long. Fold up each floret of wax around a strong, bright knitting-needle. Inserting about half the length of the small wires in each, pinch them tight. The florets are now all prepared. The next thing is the receptacle. It may be made of refuse wax, about the size of a farthing, but a quarter of an inch thick, and rounded at the upper edge. Fasten the wire for the general stem in the centre beneath, and cover the under part with numerous small green leaves, overlapping each other, for a calyx. Then choosing first the most imperfect of the florets, stick them close together near the centre, working with

them round and round, till you get to the edge, taking care to expand the cleft top of them more and more as you proceed outwards, so as to show more expanded flowers; this may be done one at a time, just before putting each one on; or, more conveniently and quickly all together at first, arranging them in this case on a table, so that they may be conveniently handled one by one when wanted. If the expanding of them has been regular, and the placing of them done neatly, the whole, when finished, will have a shape like a rather flat half ball, as the flowers naturally have.

The Lily of the Valley. — This flower must be made upon very different principles from those hitherto described. File to a round end a piece of bone, metal, plaster of Paris; or, still better, the end of a round slate-pencil; grease this end, and dip it. half an inch deep into pure white wax, so cold as to be ready to set immediately; cut it round the stick or former into five teeth. Dip it into water, when the part at the end will drop off, if assisted by the point of a penknife. This forms the bell or cup-shaped corolla. Make eight or ten of these for one branch of flowers, some rather smaller than the others, some of them also you may squeeze up into buds. Then have as many fine wires waxed with green, upon the end of each put six very small stamens of yellow. Pass up a corolla from the bottom of the stalk, and fasten it close to the stamens. Then unite the whole together into a loose bunch, the flowers drooping in the same direction. The whole must be wrapped in a leaf of bright green wax, as if it grew from the centre of it.

10 *

MODELLING OF DOUBLE FLOWERS.

ODELLING Double Flowers is infinitely more easy than that of single ones, because Nature here sports into a greater variety of shape and color. Double Flowers are of themselves unnatural, and therefore a rigid conformity with the original is by no means requisite, unless it is to be a scientific copy of some florist's variety; a deviation from which renders it valueless for the purpose intended, however handsome and well shaped. In forming Double Flowers in wax, the general form is the first consideration; also, the manner of the petals lapping over each other, and that those which come nearest to the outside of the flower are always larger than the inner ones, as well as better formed; and in a striped flower they are more decidedly and correctly streaked and

spotted. The chief favorites are the Rose, the Dahlia, the Camellia, the Carnation, Pink, Ranunculus, Anemone, and Primrose. Those flowers which are most difficult to make single, are never doubled at all, such as the Lily of the Valley, the Convolvulus, Passion Flower, and others. Instructions to form a Dahlia will be a sufficient guide for Double Flowers in general.

To form a Dahlia, choose seven sheets of the proper colored wax; and Dahlias are of every color, except black, brown, green, and blue. Cut seventy or eighty shapes with the tin guides, of which a shape is given on page 65, with some of two or three smaller sizes, keeping the various sizes separate. Coil the smallest round a wire, so as to roll them up completely. The next size must be a very little opened towards the top. The third size still more opened. The next with only the sides a trifle doubled over, and so on with the others; the outer ones being a little ribbed lengthwise, so as merely to show a waved surface; though Dahlias vary very much in this respect, most of them being somewhat quilled, even to the extreme outer row or edge. The petals being ready, take a thick wire, and place around the end of it, firmly fixing them on, some of the smallest petals; afterwards the other sizes in regular rotation; the upper surface of the whole together being of the form represented by about one third of an orange cut the flat way, or like a portion of a flattened ball. Lastly, a calyx is required; this may be of several small green leaves folding over each other, at the same time concealing the ends of the petals, and uniting them more firmly to the stem.

THE END.

THE PARLOR GARDENER.

A TREATISE ON THE HOUSE CULTURE OF ORNAMENTAL PLANTS.

Translated from the French, and adapted to American use.

BY CORNELIA J. RANDOLPH,
OF VIRGINIA.

WITH ELEVEN ILLUSTRATIVE CUTS.

Price 75 cents.

THE ART
OF
SKETCHING FROM NATURE.

TWENTY-SEVEN ILLUSTRATIONS.

Said to be the best elementary work on Drawing extant.

Price 40 cents.

SKELETON LEAVES
AND
PHANTOM FLOWERS.

A New and Practical Guide to this elegant art, the manner of skeletonizing leaves and flowers, method of grouping and arranging into bouquets. Also, guide to PRESERVING NATURAL FLOWERS with their fresh bloom and beauty.

Price, $1.50.

J. E. TILTON & CO., Publishers.

NEW DRAWING CARDS.
SKETCHING FROM NATURE FOR YOUNG ARTISTS.

A beautiful set of subjects far superior to the imported and common cards in use.

Price, per package, 50 cents.

J. E. TILTON & CO., Publishers.

JUST PUBLISHED,
WAX FLOWERS:
HOW TO MAKE THEM.

With new methods of Sheeting Wax, Modelling Fruit, &c.

Price, $1.50.

J. E. TILTON & CO., Publishers.

ART RECREATIONS.

A COMPLETE, ILLUSTRATED, AND EASY GUIDE

— TO —

Pencil Drawing, Crayon Drawing and Painting, Water-Color Painting, Oil Painting, Painters' Photographs in Water and Oil, Grecian Painting, Oriental Painting, Antique Painting, and in fact all known varieties of Drawing and Painting.

Also, Leather Work, Moss Work, Feather Work, Wax Work, Cone Work, Shell Work, &c. How to Preserve Birds, how to make Aquariums, Magic Lanterns, Papier Mache Work, Paper Flowers, Vases, &c.; in fact, a perfect Encyclopædia of all that is ornamental and useful.

To be used without a teacher; with rules for making all materials needed.

Price, muslin, ... $2.50
Half calf, ... 3.75
Rich Turkey, ... 5.00

FLOWERS

FOR THE

PARLOR AND GARDEN.

BY EDWARD SPRAGUE RAND, JR.

A splendid illustrated volume on the culture of Greenhouse, Conservatory, Stove, Parlor, and Garden Flowers, Ferns, Bulbs, &c.; Instructions and Plans on the Building, Stocking, and Keeping Conservatories, Greenhouses, &c.; Waltonian Cases, Ferneries, &c.; Soil for the Flower Garden; List of Best Plants and Seeds; How to Propagate; Time of Planting and Flowering; in short, every information needed by the amateur or the most experienced gardener. It is a volume long needed, and the author's high reputation in these matters will insure a work that will supply every want.

Price, muslin, gilt top, ... $2.75
Half calf, ... 3.75
Turkey, ... 5.00

www.ingramcontent.com/pod-product-compliance
Lightning Source LLC
Chambersburg PA
CBHW022141160426
43197CB00009B/1388